AF700807

DAILY DRAW – Portfolio II

by Mason Garrett

A journal of therapeutic drawing from past, present, and future sketch books.

DAILY DRAW – Portfolio II

As presented from 5/28/06 thru 10/12/06 at
http://www.blogit.com/Blogs/Blog.aspx/MasonGarrett/

Dedicated to my Mother, Laura Evelyn

Printed in the United States of America

ISBN 978-0-6151-3554-0

MEETING THE MUSE ON MAIN STREET...

A Sunday stroll seemed like a good way to contemplate the beginning of Portfolio II. I crossed paths with the Muse on a street corner. What parallel dimensions, separate realities, and subconscious explorations will she take us on next? ...we shall see...

Sketching in public

has always been a

relaxing and fun thing

to do

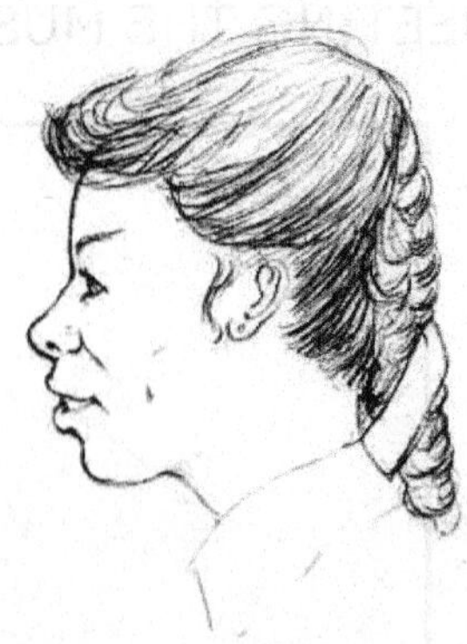

...catching

people in life

just being

people in their

everyday beauty.

EVERY FACE HAS A STORY...

The subject is a living being with a history. Their postures, faces, expressions tell that story. You listen and absorb with your psyche and your eyes and you record that story with line, shape, and shade. It's a fantastic adventure and a fascinating study. I will never tire of it and I shall continue to draw until I drop or my eyeballs quit.

TURN THE PAGE AND DRAW SOME MORE...

There are periods when I just wander about and hang out at coffee shops, malls, parks, and street corners... just watching and sketching... I call it 'people catching,' ..my version of hunting and fishing. I just don't kill them and eat them... but perhaps they are a form of psychic nourishment for me.

WE CREATE OUR OWN REALITY...

The question is... who goes first? Do I create you? Or do you create me? Or do we create each other? Me and the Muse... just goofing around... and trying to illustrate a concept... There is never a dull moment with her around.

CONTEMPLATING ON ONE'S NATURE...

There is the desire to run free... to follow instincts... Our animal side is very apparent at times. Is it any different for any of the species? They all have their nature... their responsibilities... protection of territory... the rearing of off spring... food gathering... In the end we are all food for something. Just some thoughts in the park...

WHO AND WHAT DO YOU FIND IN THE CORRIDORS OF YOUR MIND?

Who are they? And why are they hanging out in the corridors of the mind? They're not frightening... at least not here... they're just there... and some of them are rather nice...

THERE ARE MANY ROOMS IN THE MANSION OF THE MIND...

There are many rooms, many levels, many people, many memories... how deep can you go? Can you really get to all of it in one lifetime? I'm not even close to getting to the bottom of it... but the endless search and exploration is fascinating... and it always provides something interesting to draw...

GO OUTSIDE FOR AWHILE… AND SKETCH A PRETTY WOMAN…

Need to get out of the Mansion of my mind for a while… so, go out to a coffee shop and sketch some people. Here is an example of what I call a 'coffee wash.' After the quick rough sketch you dip the tip of your finger in the coffee and gently slide it through the shadow side of the face or figure. It's sort of a one shot thing… if you do it too much it all just turns to mud… but if you get it right… it looks neat and it's a lot of fun to do.

MORE WASH DRAWING...

You can also just lick the end of your finger or dip it in water... and you can get a much tighter line by using the edge of a stirring stick... or you can get professional about it and carry a small #00 sable brush in your pencil box. The main thing of course is to just have FUN with it.

TURN THE PAGE AND DO SOME MORE...

You have to be quick... on the draw... because these are people just being people and they won't sit still for a long pose. But that's the fun of it ...and of course it's a much looser style. In my youth I studied and tried to copy the quick style sketching of the French Impressionist artist Toulouse Lautrec. He was really good at it.

WHAT IS THE MUSE COOKING UP NOW?

We all have our castles in the sky... our fantasies, dreams, wishes... When the energies are balanced just right... the 4th dimension slides into the 3rd... and it manifests. My castle in the sky at the moment is my self published portfolio now in the final proofing stages... soon to be released? ...we shall see.

BACK HOME NOW... SORT OF...

Despite the complex social and political problems throughout the world... this is truly an incredible time that we're living in. I have no plan... no outline... yet day by day this art/journal/book gets drawn and written page by page... I have no idea how or why it happens... it just happens. I shall continue then... to just let it flow wherever it's going to go. I have a feeling the Muse is going to take us on a trip some where new and different. We shall see...

I DRAW… WHILE THE MUSE PETS THE BIG KITTY…

Maybe it's a wish to get out into nature more… the water, looking for the truth… the lion, looking for courage… or probably… it's just that there is this really neat banana tree near my apartment building and I just wanted to draw it… and then all of a sudden we're somewhere else… and the Muse is petting the big kitty.

WE WANDER INTO A SLEEPY RIVER TOWN...

Then we walk down river a ways and into a quiet little town. It's hot and everyone seems to be taking a nap. I've been in a rut... and this seems to be the perfect change of pace and scenery. How is it the Muse always seems to know right where I would like, or want, or need to go? She laughs after reading my thought and says, "It's just a Muse thing."

WE GO DOWN TO THE RIVER...

There is a guy with a boat there... and it seems like he is expecting us. Some journeys seem to be inevitable. This doesn't seem like the love boat nor a romantic cruse around the harbor. A bird flies overhead toward the west and the Muse just stands there silent and smiles.

JOURNEY THROUGH THE DARK...

The boatman takes us across the river into a cave filled with water. The local inhabitants aren't hostile and we aren't threatened in any way. They simply watch us in silence. Am I seeing parts of myself? ...or am I seeing my future as a very old man? Why is the boatman showing me this?

- * * * * * * * * *
  I did this drawing around Noon the past Monday, with the intention of posting it tonight... I am understandably posting it now...

The boatman had not come for me, but instead for my 87 year old mother... and she passed gently and quietly in her sleep at 12:30 AM PST ... the Sheriff Deputies have left, the paramedics carry her away... I call my relatives and now post this in her memory... the boatman came for her early today... she always was a early rising Aries...

Love you, Mom...

Yes, these drawings can be uncanny...

I shall take a few days off... and then I'll be back...

THE BOATMAN TAKES MOM INTO THE LIGHT...

Then suddenness of it all just sort of leaves me and the Muse standing here on the pier watching and wishing for her joyful journey home to the spirit of all and everything...

...the posts may be intermittent... and strange for a while as all this gets sorted out... be patient dear viewer... and thank you all, for your kind words and condolences...

ME AND THE MUSE JUST HANG OUT...

... in the basement of the mind... reviewing many subconscious memories that have been awakened recently. No regrets or guilt, just reminiscing and life review. I'm finding some interesting drawings from the 1960-70's that I had given my mother for birthday and mother's day presents. I will post some of them in the future.

TRY THIS EXPERIMENT...

Let's look at a closer crop of the last drawing.

Something different is beginning to happen. In either this or the previous view... with a relaxed soft focus of your eyes, just gaze at the Muse figure. After 15 seconds or so different areas of the drawing may appear to move slightly.. perhaps the bricks, or the figures, or the fan. The Muse figure may draw you into the picture. If you feel this shift in awareness... try to just flow with it and into the picture... pour of cup of tea and join us at the table... and maybe have an adventure with us in this parallel reality.

I will be very interested in your experiences and responses, do please respond, dear viewer...

MOTHERS... GOD BLESS THEM... THEY SAVE EVERYTHING...

A bridge over a canal somewhere in Holland in 1967... I came across some old drawings that my mother had saved. I sent them to her from Europe from time to time as birthday, mother's day, and Christmas presents.

Hiedelberg Bridge, Germany

DRAWINGS THAT I SENT HOME DURING MY US ARMY SERVICE AND WHILE I WAS STATIONED IN WEST GERMANY 1966-68

"Hi Mom & Dad, The army let's me drive a really cool sports car...

..and we go on a lot of camping trips near the East German border to deter the Soviets from invading Europe..."

I LIVED IN A 700 YEAR OLD CASTLE...

Families that have inherited large estates and castles often convert the old battlements, towers, arms room, etc. into modern cozy studio apartments to help pay the high taxes and maintenance costs.. This is a drawing of the upstairs castle tower apartment that I rented in Friedberg, Germany for three months in 1970. It was one of the most comfortable little studios that I have ever had.

CAMPFIRE, SMOKE, SHADOWS... MEMORIES...

Me and the Muse have an evening of reflection. What is the sum of one's life? What have I learned? You were all there for some reason as I was for some reason in your life. What have we given each other? What more can we give? More and more I experience life as an incredible and marvelous mystery, puzzle, and adventure... what more is to come? ..just questions on a warm evening in the woods.

THE ADVENTURE CONTINUES...

I have no idea what the Muse has in mind or where this series of drawings are headed. I just saw some interesting pictures of some pyramids in Mexico and the Muse said, "okay, let's go."

...and so.. here we are.

TIME AND DIMENSION TAVEL...

Me and the Muse drink some refreshing mango juice and have a fascinating conversation with Quetzalcoatl, this reptile-bird like fellow, out on the patio of the pyramid penthouse. He explained that through the use of different types of a vortex, one could travel to whatever location and time period you choose. He also said that there were a few vortex tunnels inside the pyramid if we would like to try it.

MAGDALENE PICKS A VORTEX...

Our host, Quetzalcoatl, the reptile-bird fellow, gives us a guided tour of the various chambers and rooms inside the pyramid. The Muse chooses a purple vortex. Me and Quetzalcoatl exchange pleasantries and email addresses and she goes skipping down the corridor toward the vortex. Most of the time she is Magdalene the Muse, a beautiful mother earth like Goddess that I love with all my being... today she has been Maggie the teen who just has to see and ride everything in Pyramid Park... so, I guess we're going to ride the Purple Vortex now...

THE PURPLE VORTEX... WHAT A RIDE! ... YAHOO!

It's that first step that sort of takes your breath away. The Muse is really good at this inter-dimensional flying thing. I'm still sort of clumsy at it and I do more falling and tumbling than controlled and conscious flying ...and I usually land in a heap. Quetzalcoatl said this vortex hasn't been used for awhile, and that he wasn't quite sure, but he thinks it ends up somewhere in the Orient... we shall see...

COOL LANDING... WE CHILL AND DRY OUT...

We landed in a creek in the woods. It's warm, quiet, and we enjoy being wet for a while. Ever since the vortex turned left outside of Albuquerque, I've been totally lost and I have no idea what century it may be. But I'm with the Muse and she doesn't seem too concerned about it. I think that's her main lesson to me... go with the flow... don't worry... be happy... and just BE... and if you be wet... BE wet...

WE MEET A FELLOW TRAVELER...

Me and the Muse put on some coffee and cook up some snacks... and all of a sudden this Chinese cowboy rides in on his water buffalo. I invite him over for a rest and a cup of java. He accepts and introduces himself as Lao Tzu, a freelance writer, poet, philosopher, shaman, mystic.... who is just passing through and on his way to the West China desert

LAO TZU INVITES US TO DINNER AT A LOCAL ROADSIDE DINER...

After a delicious dinner we get into a discussion about the current chaos in Zhou Dynasty (1122-226 BCE)... I figured we were in a different century, what with no signs posted in the woods about campfire permits and no park rangers snooping around. Lao Tzu had been working as an archivist in the Imperial Library of the Zhou Dynasty, to support himself while he worked on his major book 'Tao Te Ching.' The political situation got so bad that he just up and quit his job at the Imperial Library, saddled up his water buffalo, and split... and headed out toward the West China desert to find some peace and quiet and cleaner air... where he could concentrate on his writing. But... just up the road is the border to the desert and at the Hangu custom post, he was asked by Yin Xi, an officer of the post, to leave his philosophy in writing before departing into the desert. And we complain about wire tapping! In the Zhou Dynasty they made you put it in writing! ...and that was why he had been out in the woods for a few days... writing it all down for this tinhorn official so he could be on his way to his desert retreat and back to the writing that he really wanted to do.

We didn't have to ask. He ask us to read the scroll that he had written for the official ...and that he would appreciate some feedback and discussion... do we think it will get him through the border check point? ...or is it too anti-government?

This is heavy stuff! ...and the parallels to our current political situation are simply uncanny, for instance here he says, "Why are people starving? Because the rulers eat up the money in taxes. Therefore the people are starving." ...and here, all the marches and demonstrations lately, "Why are people rebellious? Because the rulers interfere too much. Therefore they are rebellious." And just like our current voter apathy, "Why do people think so little of death? Because the rulers demand too much of life. Therefore people take life lightly." ...sure enough... as they go strapping on bombs and blowing themselves and others to pieces.

The amazing simplicity.. by 'doing nothing' one could 'accomplish everything.' And he writes,

> "The Tao abides in non-action,
> Yet nothing is left undone.
> If kings and lords observed this,
> The ten thousand things would develop naturally,
> If they still desired to act,
> They would return to the simplicity of formless substance.
> Without form there is no desire.
> Without desire there is tranquility.
> In this way all things would be at peace."

Wouldn't it be great if this guy ran for president on a 3rd party independent ticket!

My favorite quote is, "The Taoist has no ambitions, therefore he can never fail. He who never fails always succeeds. And he who always succeeds is all-powerful."

After reading it, all I could say was, "Dude.. right on! ...go for it!" ...and then I added, "don't worry about the border... if your times are as corrupt as mine, all you have to do is roll up a C-note in the scroll when you give it to him... you'll get across, no problem."

THE MUSE HELPS LAO TZU WHILE I SKETCH…

We order another pot of green tea while Lao Tzu and the Muse go over some of his rough draft for his book the, TAO TE CHING. She helps him come up with some subtle imagery that he likes… and I'm just soaking it all in and sketching some of the locals that are hanging out here at the roadside diner.

...BACK TO SAN GABRIEL...

Me and the Muse see Lao Tzu off to his rendezvous with the border guard and then make camp again in the woods. How to get home again? Well, you can click the heels of your ruby slippers three times and chant "There's no place like home, there's no place like home..." or you can step into a magic phone booth and dial the appropriate area code, or you can dial in the appropriate date into a complicated H.G. Wells time machine, or you can do the same with a 'Back to the Future,' Delorian sports car, or you can do a sling shot orbit around the Sun in a Starship at warp-8.... or, as Quetzalcoatl pointed out, you can draw and focus on a clockwise vortex... and whoosh! ...we're back in San Gabriel.

GET BACK TO HERE AND NOW…

I've been cooped up in this apartment for a week or two… time to get outside again… and in this dimension… There's always a pretty woman to sketch somewhere and I go looking and find this lovely young woman having a donut at a little coffee shop around the corner.

THERE ARE ALWAYS LOTS OF PEOPLE TO DRAW...

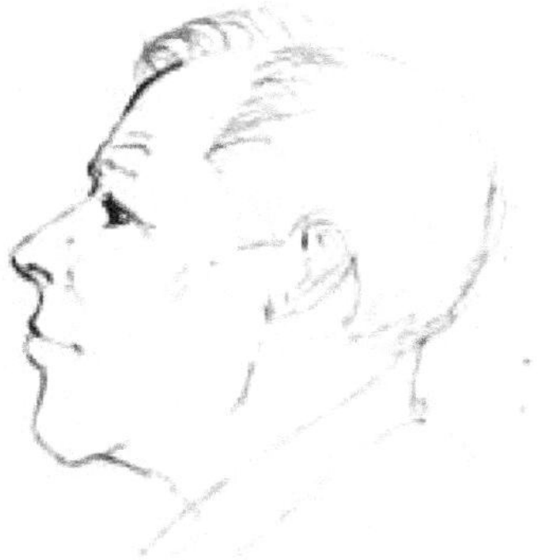

I'm in that mood to just wander around here and there and to just hang out and draw whoever shows up. It gets me away from my personal problems. Life is a complex puzzle for us all with many issues and you can see that in the various the faces, postures, and gestures of those around you. We all feel different and unique... yet in so many ways were all the same... and we are all connected.

HAVE YOU EVER SEEN THIS FELLOW?

Did you ever have a boss, teacher, uncle, neighbor, or maybe friend who looked like this fellow? For some reason I feel intuitively I know this person... and he's frustrated about something... Sometimes there is a powerful exchange with the people I draw... like there is some kind of a psychic connection.

A COUPLE OF FELLOWS DISCUSS LAST NIGHT'S BALL GAME...

...or maybe the election issues, the lousy economy, work problems, social problems, opinions, relationship problems, gossip... people simply talk to each other in coffee shops ...there is a need... an energy there that we want/need... they've been around for thousands of years... coffee shops, diners, inns, ...or just wherever the people can gather and reach out, connect, and exchange energy with one another... hopefully in a compassionate and loving way... there is always that opportunity and choice to and make... we create our own reality ... the good, the bad, and the ugly... and now, my friend, what shall we eat/drink and talk/exchange about?

ANOTHER PRETTY WOMAN...

I am having exceptional luck lately in catching pretty profiles and pleasant conversation,

"Are you drawing me?"

"Yes, I hope you don't mind.... Are you a Capricorn?"

"...Why... yes... how did you know that?"

"High cheek bones, chiseled classic features...quiet, yet confident manner..."

"Are you an Astrologer as well as an artist?"

"Yes, I am"

...AND ON THROUGH THE AFTERNOON.. .SKETCHING PEOPLE...

I try to draw honestly with ... no selection... no judgment... I just draw whoever shows up for as long as they will let me get away with it. Sometimes and in some strange way... even though they are all total strangers... I seem to know them all...

Like... we are all connected....

...AND WHEN NOBODY IS AROUND...

You're stuck with drawing whatever is in front of you...

That can be...

..an interesting experiment in accepting the NOW...

and the IS...

... of the moment ... and of the situation...

BUT… IF I'M DRAWING THE PARKING LOT…

…then maybe…

it's time for me to go home…

OTHER DIMENSIONS OPEN AGAIN...

As I walk across the parking lot and observe the traffic going by I have another one of those strange shifts in awareness. This drawing is from 1988 when it first started to occur. Now when it occurs it is starting to have physical sensations. I felt a tingling sort of buzz in the middle of my upper back between the shoulder blades. Then in a moment the fabric of my ordinary reality seems to rip open and I am seeing and being in other places. While the experience seems to last for a few minutes... in my ordinary reality it is only for a few seconds, this time in the space of taking two or three steps toward my truck. Then in a few moments everything is back and I'm setting in my truck pondering, '...what was that all about?' Fortunately it has never occurred during heavy traffic or while doing any physical labor with tools.

I would like to develop some sort of control over it... but it never seems to happen that way when I try and do it on purpose.

Strange phenomenon...

HAUNTED STREETS?

Some streets in South Pasadena feel haunted to me. It's an area of Los Angeles that I've always enjoyed and felt comfortable in. Someday I may move back there. For some reason I feel very at home there and it's easy to slip back in time and see scenes and people. Lately when hanging out there I have felt/seen scenes from the 1940's. I have drawn this 1942 Plymouth before but never at this angle nor with a woman dressed in this style. Maybe I've been watching too much film noir lately. There was a time when a lady with a hat on that size could sit in a car and drive it.

AN ANCIENT PARABLE

The philosopher and mystic G.I. Gurdjieff would often tell this parable to his students. I will paraphrase it as best I can. In this life we are entrusted with three things, a wolf, a sheep, and a cabbage and we must get them all across the river of life intact. There is only a small boat which is just big enough to carry oneself and one of the three things. Somehow one must get all three across the river of life without the wolf eating the sheep, or the sheep eating the cabbage. They represent the three sides of ourselves, the physical instinctive side, the emotional side, and the intellectual side. If we are too intellectual, the emotions and physical side are neglected. If we are too emotional we are irrational and do things to harm the body. If we satisfy only our physical needs the mind is neglected and we have no conscience. The riddle isn't difficult. First you take the sheep across because the wolf won't eat the cabbage. Then when you come back, do you get the wolf or the cabbage? If you take the wolf and leave it with the sheep, the wolf will eat the sheep. If you take the cabbage and leave it, the sheep will eat the cabbage. So, You take the wolf across... and then your must bring the sheep back. Then you take the cabbage across and come back again to get the sheep a second time. The point is, in one's effort to evolve as a human, one must make and 'extra,' effort by self observation and awareness. Am I being too emotional and making an unwise decision? Am I being too intellectual and forgetting about my feelings? Am I neglecting my body and instincts? Are my physical wants damaging my body? To be a balanced, sane, compassionate, and loving person takes an extra effort... self examination, awareness, and conscious choices are required to get all three sides of ourselves across the river of life intact without one devouring the other.

We have all been at various times everywhere in this parable. We are or have known exciting but dangerous wolves. Sometimes in our thinking we simply go along with the herd... or we're as dumb as a cabbage. Or we're frightened sheep or over logical sunlight seeking cabbages... and we're rowing like crazy trying to keep it all together... without something getting eaten... or the boat getting tipped over.

HAVE YOUR EVER FELT BAITED... AND BETRAYED?

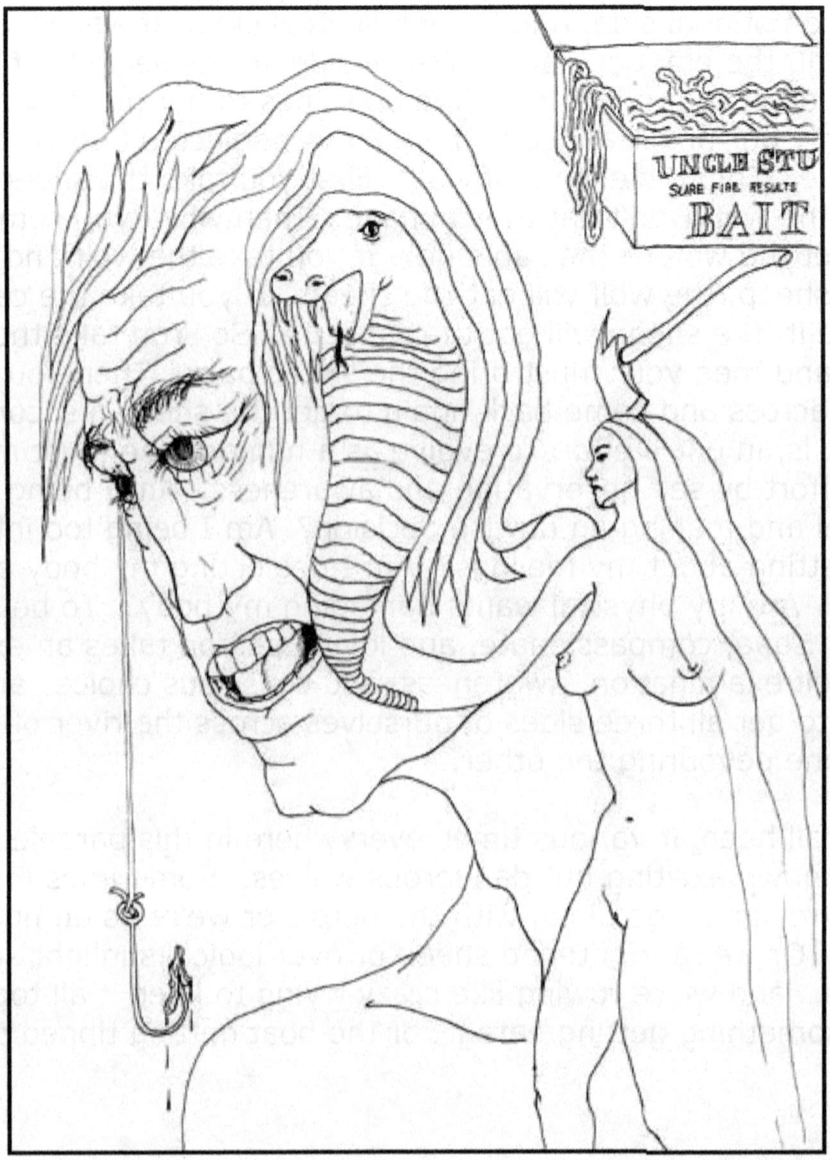

This is a drawing from 1987 during my psycho therapy sessions after a nervous breakdown. It's not a pretty drawing but it was very necessary for therapy to somehow release the rage created by betrayal from trusted friends and the resulting physical assault during an armed burglary that nearly killed me and put me on disability for over a year. Rage is not an easy thing to deal with. When one's inner animal is wounded it can very dangerous to itself and all those near it. As horrible as it may be... this is one of the most therapeutic drawings I ever did. Through this drawing and many others of that time I managed to release most of the anger. Most of them were so horrible that I later tore them up.

MEDICATION CAN PUT THE RAGE TO SLEEP... BUT NOT RELEASE IT...

Medications like Xanx and Librium can put a lid on the rage... but they don't stop the dreams. Four years of service in any branch of the military can teach one many lethal techniques of vengeance. Premeditated murder, or drug abuse, ...or therapy... you have to make choices and then live with the results. Therapy is better. If you need it, look for it, it's available in many forms. I chose drawing and so far it has worked for me... many times.

EVERYONE HAS THEIR TIME...

Mr. Bones taps us all eventually. How does one go out? Do you go out a screaming, frightened, blithering idiot... or do you go out like a warrior with calm acceptance of the inevitable? You live, you make choices, experience the results, learn your lessons... give it your best shot... and leave it go at that...

TIME FOR SOME SOCIAL LIFE...

All this therapy stuff is getting kind of heavy... time to go out and lighten up for awhile. Toulouse Lautrec had the Moulon Rouge club... and in this reality I have the Black Angus bar... and we both have a looser style of drawing with a couple of three drinks. You can tell from the faces... this is happy hour.

HAVING FUN WITH A WHISKY WASH...

Adding a wash with a finger tip using whisky or rum works as well as coffee. Canadian Club with Coke seems to work the best for me. Gin or Vodka blurs too much... is it a chemical reaction to the paper, or my brain? ...I suspect it's the latter. The fellow in the upper corner is making some good eye contact... and the fellow in the lower corner obviously isn't saying what the lady wants to hear. People enjoy quick sketch souvenirs... and quite often they pay for my drink... ...cheers...

WHAT TO DO NOW?

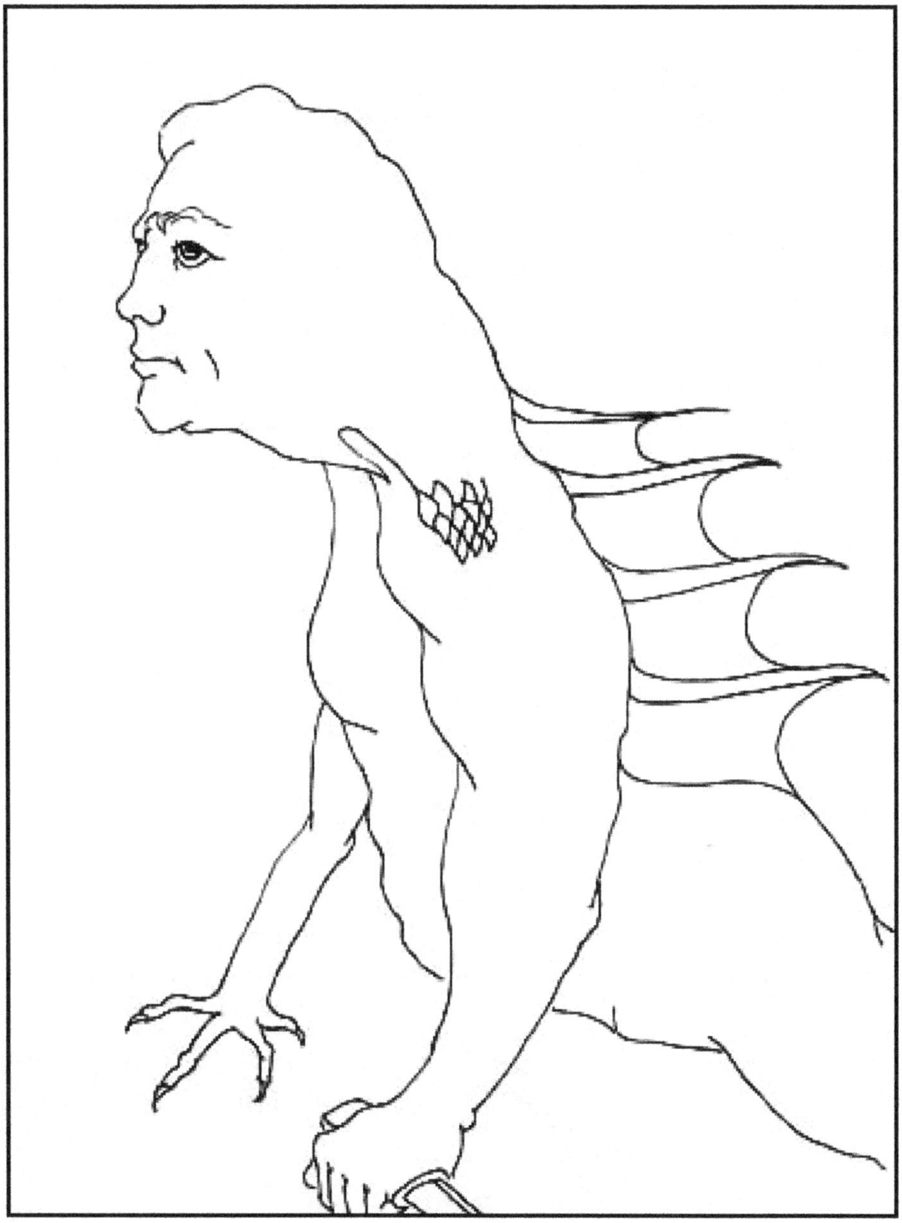

Therapy and self examination shows one the various sides of oneself. On going scientific research reveals traces of all the past species, since we crawled up out of the slime millions of years ago, to be somewhere in our DNA structure. Does one choose to wallow in the slime... or to strive to evolve to the higher?

FEELING THE CONNECTION...

Sometimes the connections are very strong... at other times they fade out and I have trouble even remembering my phone number. At other times I hear thoughts, see images of people, and I wonder are they simply memories... or am I tuning into others... or by accident getting connected with others. It's not like I can sit down and choose, 'okay, what is Mary Ann up to?'...that would be psychic snooping. Yet sometimes just out of the blue... I do know what she's up to... Strange phenomenon, I just wish I understood it more.

IF YOU'RE LUCKY... YOU CAN SHARE IN SOME TENDER MOMENTS...

Our culture has some very twisted views of sex and relationships... filled with ego, seduction, lies... we all struggle through the ugliness of it... at one time or another.

In my senior years it becomes clearer... and it's so simple... If I come from the heart chakra and simply project, and sincerely mean, the thought... 'I love you,' ..and then just let it go... it's truly amazing how people sometimes respond. ...and if they don't... does it really matter? ...at least you're free from the lies.

ESCAPE AND EVASION...

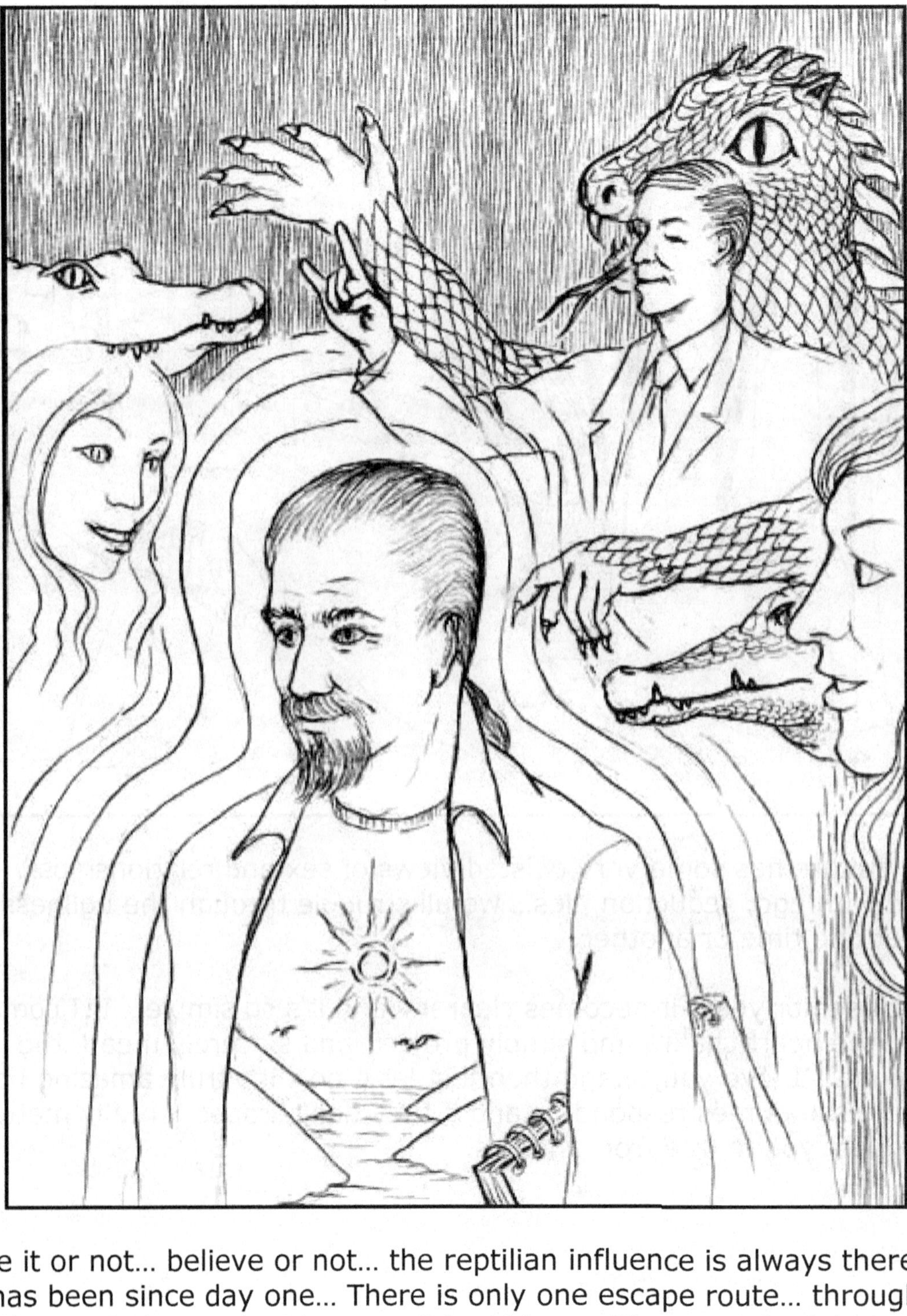

Like it or not... believe or not... the reptilian influence is always there... It has been since day one... There is only one escape route... through the heart chakra and with unconditional love... They just don't know how to deal with it... and in the end that's what it all is... infinite love.

DIFFERENT POINTS OF VIEW…

We all have a 'point of view' from where ever one is standing or sitting…whose point of view is 'right?' …What platform do you stand for/on?… is it politically 'correct?' Every day people argue and even kill one another over 'points of view,' or political 'platforms,' or religious 'views,'…It's just a silly picture…optical illusions… perhaps it is all just an… illusion… and maya of the mind?

ME AND THE MUSE PEEK ON THE OTHER SIDE OF THE VEIL...

At times the fabric of the universe seems really rather flimsy... and it's our minds with their opinions, beliefs, prejudices and convictions that make it all as hard as cement. In a relaxed meditative state one can see the 1940's, the pyramid, crocodiles down by the river, or just where or whatever you want. It all seems to be connected somehow to this loopy ladder DNA thing... sort of like a DVD movie that you can fast forward or rewind to whatever point you want.

THE MUSE WANTS TO TAKE A BREAK FROM THIS HEAVY STUFF...

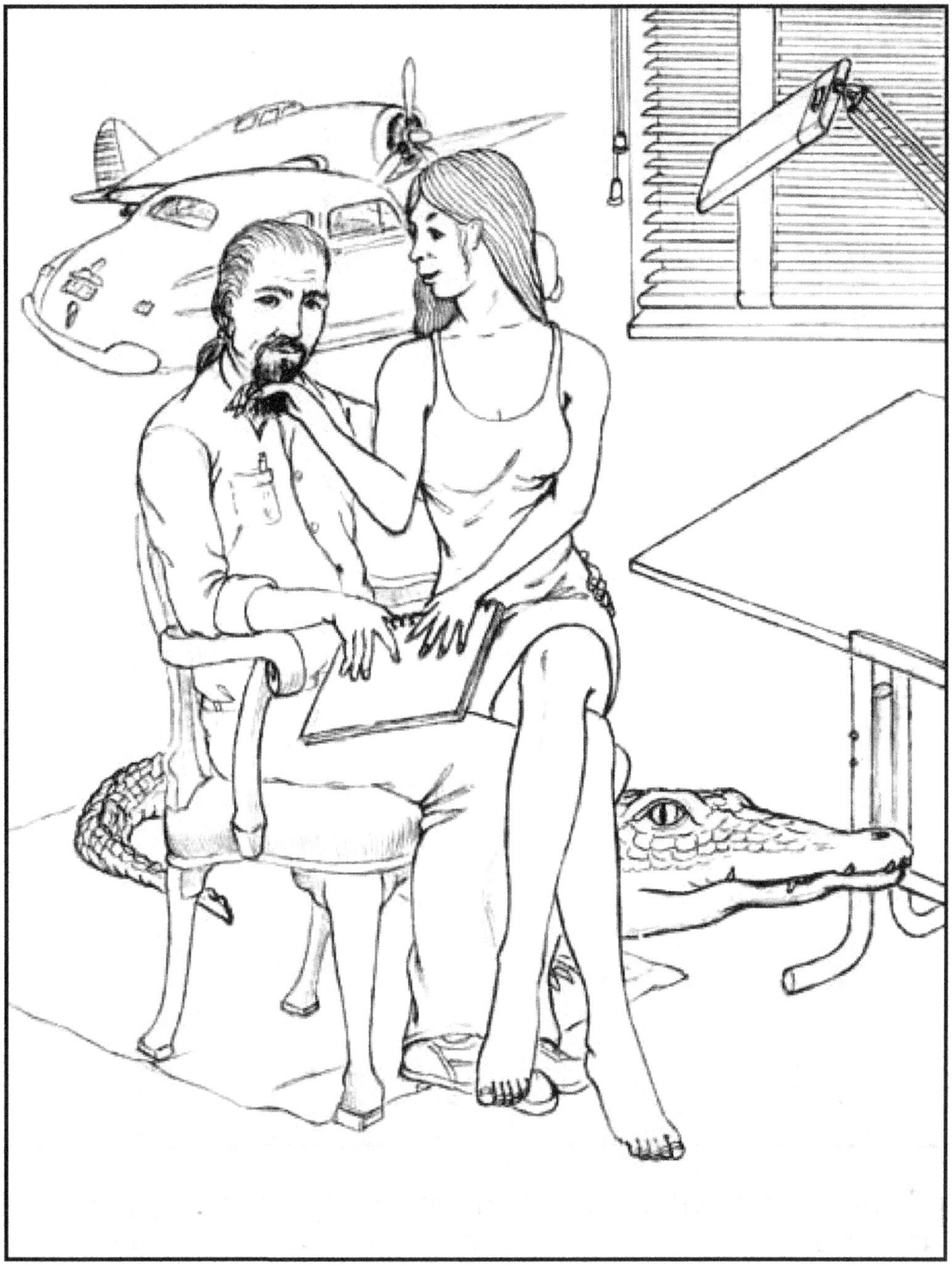

I was ready to draw something deep and profound with a really neat antique chair, a 1940 Plymouth Coupe, an early P-47 Thunderbolt pursuit plane, and maybe another crocodile... but it's really hot... and the Muse has suggested that we go out to the local A & W for an ice cold root beer float... so we're going to go chill out and draw outside for a while.

CONTENTMENT CAN BE AS SIMPLE AS CRACKERS IN ONE'S SOUP...

I often find the real art to be outside among the ordinary people of life... like this fellow... late at night in a diner... maybe he just got off work... or maybe he just can't sleep and goes out for a while... whatever... and in the moment he knows exactly what he wants... crackers broken up in his bowl of tomato soup. It makes as much sense as anything else...

CONTEMPLATION IN A COFFEE SHOP...

...'why doesn't he call?...why do I put up with this? ...I've dumped better men than this jerk! ...what is this thing I have for him? ...he doesn't care... he's off with that floozy... I know he is... maybe I should just go back to school... get my certification... that's the smart thing to do... but, but...

...who is that guy over there? ...is he drawing me?'

I AM SMITTEN! ...A BRIEF COFFEE SHOP ROMANCE...

...She was there just long enough for me to catch this... she didn't mind posing... she seemed to enjoy it... then she got a call on her cell phone and left... and I had to work the details from memory...

...oh, well... no regrets... she was an absolute treasure... and for a brief moment I made passionate love to her... with a pencil... I am indeed a lucky fellow....

AN EARLY MASON GARRETT... AGE 5... THE FIRE ENGINE AT WORK.

I found this as I went through my late mother's mementos. There was a fire in our neighborhood that I witnessed... and then later in the evening I drew my impressions of it... all little fellows draw fire engines... just because... they're really neat!

ONE OF MY FIRST PORTRAITS…

No 5 year old artist's portfolio is complete without a portrait of BUGS BUNNY

THE BRIC-A-BRAC OF ONE'S LIFE...

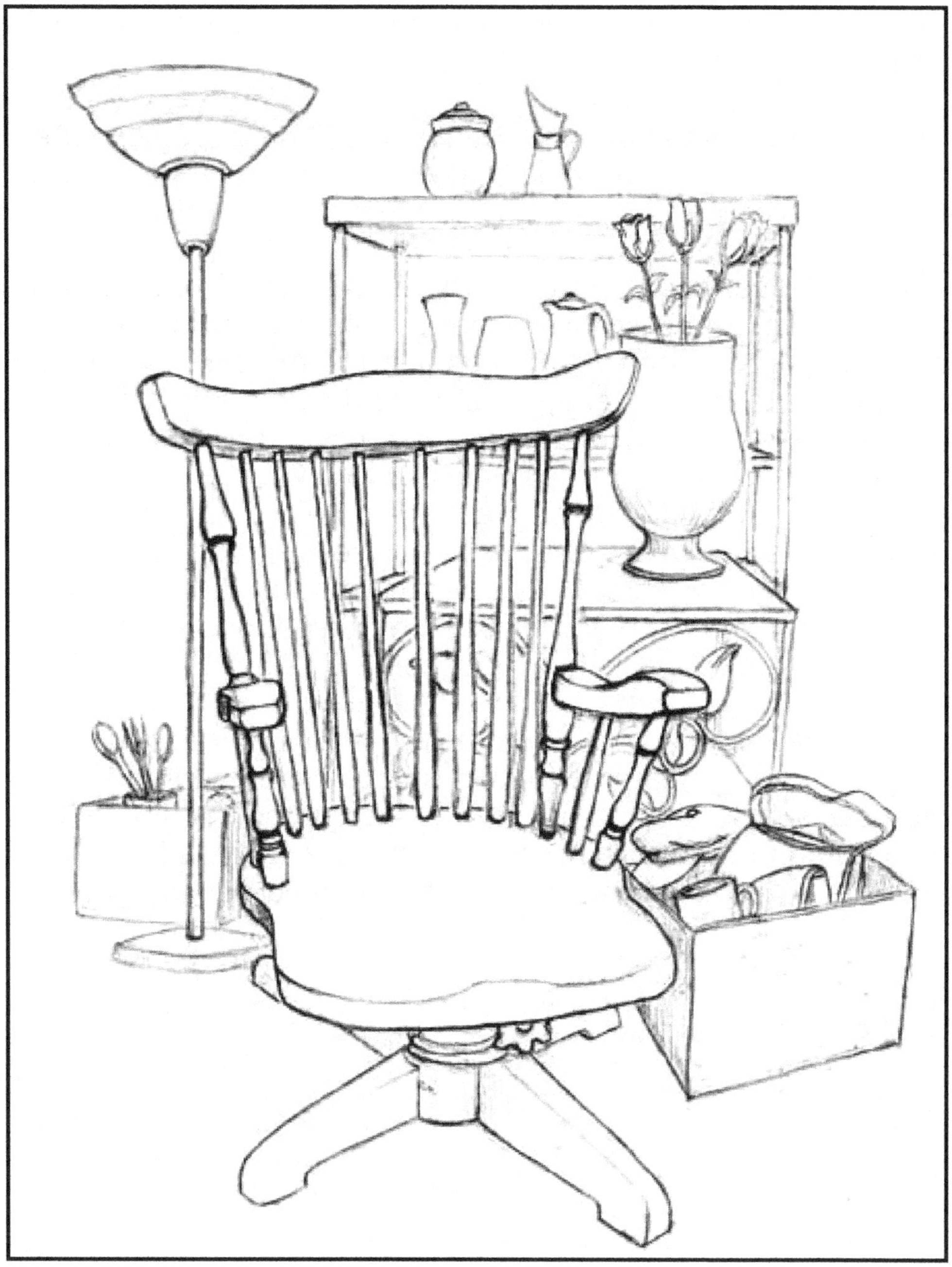

This has been a difficult, but very necessary, and therapeutic drawing for me to do... and being that this is a therapeutic drawing, it has to be published. I practice what I preach and in this drawing I have finally found peace and closure with the passing of my mother this past June 12th. The old cliché, 'You can't take it with you,' becomes blaringly obvious when a family member dies... you're stuck with their stuff. During her 87 years my mother accumulated a lot... and this drawing is only one corner of the room and it is what is left after relatives and friends have gone through it all and taken what they can comfortably fit into their life.

Yes, of course I have kept some things like photos, personal items, and childhood drawings of mine that she has lovingly kept tucked away all these years.

However, the over two hundred plastic flowers and thrift store vases to keep them in, odd ceramic statuettes, elephants, miniature spoons from various states... it is all just too much of an emotional burden for me to keep around. Just seeing some of this silly stuff brings me to tears in odd moments... like now... I do need to put it aside now and get on with what is left of my life. So I will make a drawing or two of it all and this weekend a very dear friend who conducts yard sales will relieve me of the rest of it... where yet another person will accumulate it... as my mother did... God bless her... she was a yard sale and thrift store junkie... I pass no judgment, nor do I complain... I suppose it was her form of therapy.

It is an inspiration in a way. I am hoping that I have enough warning so as to liquidate my affairs and to be laying in a Veteran's hospital bed with nothing more than a sketch book and a pencil when it's time for me to check out... and if there should be a pretty nurse... one last pretty face to draw... that would be nice...

ESCAPE FROM WOLVES, CRCODILLES, & SURVALIANCE CAMERAS...

Everybody seems to be howling about something, or some crocodile creditor is trying to eat you, or some government official or hacker is spying on you. It's been a bit stressful so the Muse and I are going to do some Vortex time tripping for awhile. These drawings are meant to be meditative visual aids to stimulate creative imagination with conscious intent... just for the fun of it... or for whatever you want.

WE ARRIVE AT THE GALATIC VORTEX TERMINAL...

No haphazard falling/flying through vortexes this time... At the top of the long stairway is the Muse's Pitcarin PCA-2 Autogiro (Circa 1931) fitted with the latest state of the art inter-dimensional instruments and guidance systems... so she says... I haven't the foggiest idea what she is talking about and I suspect she is shinning me on and that this is going to be yet another of our wild "by-the-seat-of-our-pants," adventures. What is she getting me into now?

BACK TO THE BIG APPLE... Circa 1930's...

The Autogiro was a really good idea on the Muse's part. The 1930's Manhattan is not a place you want to just fall out of a vortex into. There were newspaper reporters and photographers waiting when we landed on an open spot down by the docks. It was the era of Charles Lindbergh, Amelia Earhart, Wiley Post and other dare devil pilots and when I said we were from San Gabriel, California, they just assumed that we had made a record cross country flight to New York. So we let them assume (simply because who would believe the real story?) and they put us up in this really fancy hotel for free! It's seems that if you own a Pitcarin PCA-2 Autogiro in 1931... that means you're really cool! The headlines read, **THE DARING DUO, MAGGIE AND MASON, CROSS THE COUNTRY IN AUTOGIRO!**

WORK AND FUN... CREATIVE VISUALIZATION EXERCISE...

Follow and flow with the images... Work vs. Fun... Why not have both?

What would be fun? ..flying around in the Pitcarin PCA-2 Autogyro!
What would be fun work? ...getting paid to fly around at air shows and at carnivals!

So... soon we have an agent and we're booked at local air shows and carnivals... where we demonstrate the maneuverability and the short take off and landing capabilities of the Pitcarin PCA-2 Autogyro. Yahoo!

AND AT NIGHT... WE PLAY SOME MORE...

There's always something fun to do in Manhattan... Terrific Nightclubs where you could see a good show and then dine and drink (at certain places only, it was still during the Prohibition era) and dance the night away...

With our new income we expanded our wardrobe so as to fit in better with the time period. So, we finally see the Muse in a new dress... and with shoes on! ...and I'm even wearing something besides my usual denims.

...how sweet it is!

WE DON'T WANT TO CHANGE HISTORY, SO WE BETTER SPLIT...

Soon the press revealed that another pilot, John Miller, actually flew the first transcontinental flight with an autogyro a few days before we arrived on the scene. We just got more publicity than he did. We graciously concede the record to him and quietly begin to pack our things before someone gets wise to the vortex thing.

We announce to the press that we will attempt a record flight between New York and Rio de Janeiro... and then we head out toward the Bermuda Triangle area and turn into the first vortex we find... and then poof! ...we're one of the hundreds of aircraft and ships that have suddenly disappeared without a trace in that mysterious area... and then wooooosh! ...we're at the pyramids in Yucatan, Mexico. It seems that vortex energies have something to do with pyramids.

PROBLEMS WITH LOGICAL THINKING...

As it often happens with time travel... you're not quite sure what day or century you've just popped into. There are no road signs or souvenir shops around indicating a pre-1900 AD era to be most likely... but what era? Who's in charge here the Mayans, or Cortes, or Poncho Villa?

There doesn't seem to be anyone around and we start to explore the pyramid looking for a less conspicuous place to park the Pitcarin PCA-2 Autogiro... and maybe find some accommodations and a cantina... and we go down some steps at a side entrance and find this huge well lighted basement room under the pyramid.

I've never seen the Muse in such a state of awe. As you know by now, I have a thing for old cars and motorcycles... and, well... her hobby is the restoration and flying of antique aircraft... and here parked under this pyramid is a vast array of old airplanes... many of which probably took the wrong vortex off ramp out on the Bermuda Triangle Galactic Freeway Interchange.

She soon has her heart set on a Grumman TBF Avenger Torpedo-Bomber... a lot more luggage space is her suggestion. I suggest there might be problems going back to 2006 with it... like it belongs to the US Navy... and they will probably want to know what we are doing with one of their torpedo-bombers from WWII! What are we going to tell them... we just found it parked under a pyramid in Mexico? Then we'll have the DEA, ATF, FBI, and CIA, and their dope dogs sniffing around all over it... you know how these government people are... I am experiencing some anxiety now.

She gives me a reassuring hug... kisses my cheek... and whispers, "Not to worry, love ...I have a plan... it will be fun... you'll see... trust me.."

FUN AT THE AIR SHOW...

We roll the Pitcarin PCA-2 Autogryro down to the basement and trade it for the Grumman TBF Avenger Torpedo-Bomber. She switches her small computers from one cockpit to the other. I move our bags... and she was right... there is a lot more room in the old bomb racks for our new luggage from New York. Then she types some data into her small computer and we taxi into the vortex at the end of the big basement room and ...wooosh! ...we fly out of San Gabriel canyon and head toward the Chino, California Airfield where we land and register as an entry into the Saturday airshow... and then we have fun flying around with other pilots who also collect, restore, and fly antique aircraft.

Yes, I have had the same questions you have... how does she do all of this? ...and I ask her, "We always get right in, no problem, how is it you always seem to have all the right forms and answers the officials want to see and hear?"

And she answers, "People want to have it be 'right' in their reality... so, I peek into their head and find the memories of the forms and words they want to see and hear... and then simply play it back for them in their head... like a videotape or DVD... and they see and hear what they want... even though they're really looking at a blank piece of paper from your sketch book... and then we get to go play with the airplane... simple stuff really..."

That part I follow... but here's where I get confused... we left the Galactic Vortex Terminal in the Pitcarin PCA-2 Autogyro Tuesday August 1, 2006... we fly into Manhattan in the year of 1931... and week or so later we leave there and arrive in Yucatan Mexico... I have no idea when... and then we fly out of that vortex in a Grumman TBF Avenger Torpedo-Bomber and into the Chino airshow of July 29, 2006... four days before we left! ...and down in the corner of my computer screen it reads Monday, August 8, 2006... Trying to figure this out... is making my head hurt... I'm going to smoke a bowl now... and then go to bed...and hope that I wake up... at the right time tomorrow.

TIME TO GO OUSIDE... AND SKETCH SOME REAL PEOPLE...

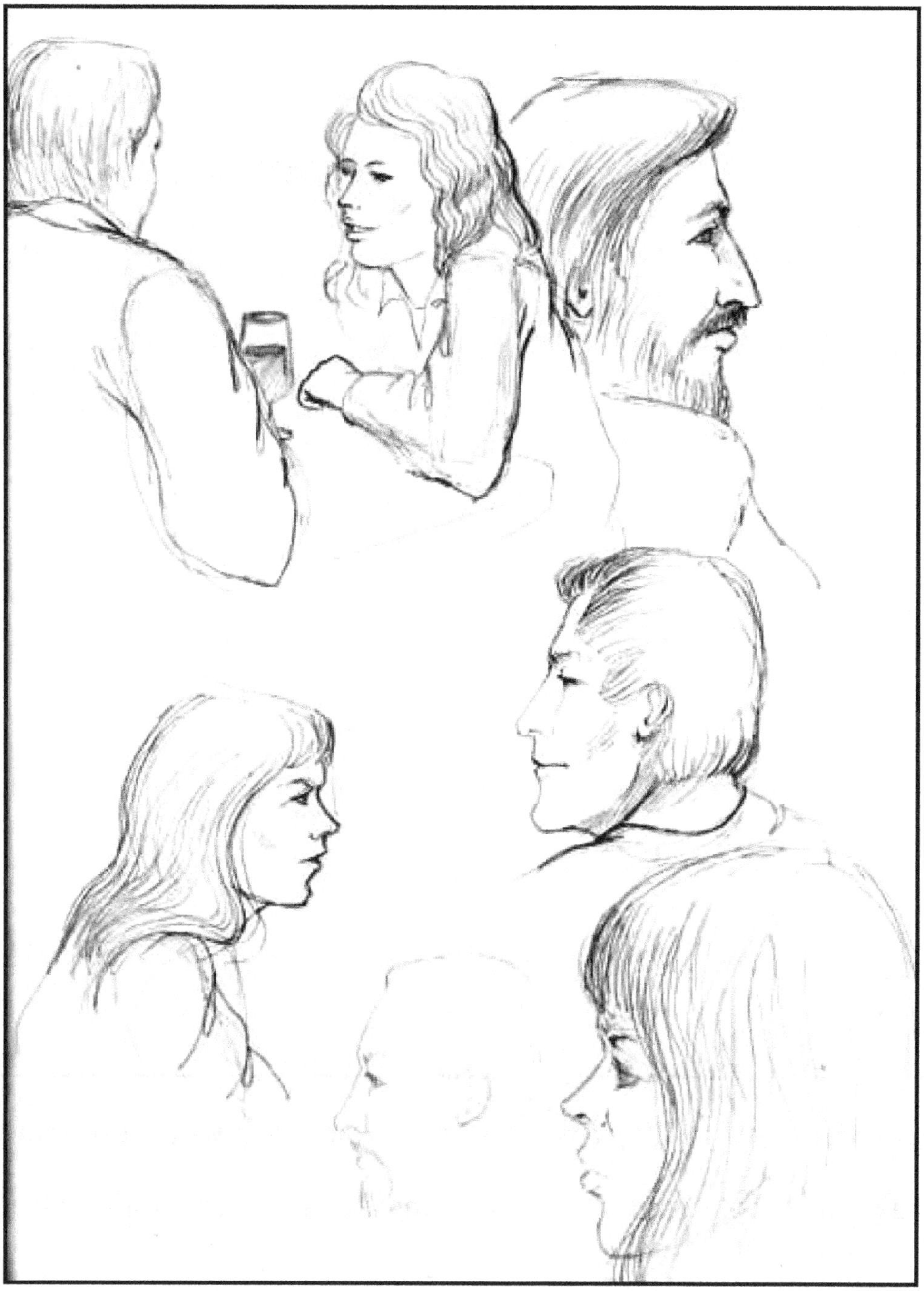

We can get caught up in our own personal world and fantasy escapes. I let these past few days just take off into ideas that I've wanted to draw... old airplanes... different realities... now it's time to come back and deal with my own world... as it is now... in this coffee shop.

SOMEHOW I DON'T THINK SHE BELIEVES HIM...

Sometimes I feel like I'm eavesdropping... and in a way I probably do...

People's postures, gestures, expressions... often speak volumes... and I listen with a pencil...

HE'S BUSTED...AND TRYING TO THINK OF SOMETHING FAST...

"I saw you with her... out in the parking lot!"

"I was just saying hello..."

"With your arm around her!"

"She's just a friend... it was nothing..."

"...and the tongue kiss? ...oh, yes... very friendly!"

A CUTE SCORPIO... AND OTHER PEOPLE WITH ATTITUDES...

Maybe their horoscopes are all crossed up for today... and some of the people at this diner seem to have attitudes and issues...

Then this cute little Scorpio lady... Lisa is her name... sits down at the counter next to me... and just makes my day...

THE MUSE IS NUDGING ME ON TO SOME MORE DIMENSION TRAVEL...

Lately I've been using an Elestial Quartz Crystal, a five inch point of six planes; on the point are six triangular planes, and six rectangular sides. Scrying is the ancient art of interring a meditative state by gazing with a relaxed focus into any shiny surface. I hold the crystal in my lap and then gaze on one of the possible twelve basic planes with a reflecting light.

With a mind that is vibrating concentration energy though conscious focus with intent one can switch one's consciousness to another parallel dimension or reality, sometimes as a passive observer like watching a play of live actors... or by astraly entering the plane as a full participant in the game park... The crystal's different planes seem to be various entries or channels, like on a television... and you can select what you want to view or experience. It usually takes about ten minutes of gazing for me to reach a state where this can happen... the trick is to stay relaxed and calm... and just say, 'okay, let's go on the ride,' embrace your dharma, and try to live it with unconditional love... It can be a lot of fun.

Just about any shiny surface will do, but not enough to over strain the eye, the reflected light of a nearby lamp will do, candles if you like them or practice candle magick. Be as creative with your ritual as you like... it's your ritual... and it's scared between you and the Supreme Being of your choice... many spokes lead to the same wheel...

During a recent session of gazing, the Muse and I got some helpful hints from a local wizard on how to focus the crystal into shaper and multiple pictures. On our first try we got two different lives going on simultaneously yet in different centuries... This fellow James is living in 1228 A.D. and is with the Knights Templar... and in 1945 he is a WWII, P-51 Mustang fighter pilot, flying missions over Nazi Germany... we evidently live multiple lives... all the time... past, present, future all happening now... and you can be aware of more than one of them...at any time... when you're ready to allow for the possibility of it...

INVITATION TO ANOTHER TIME...

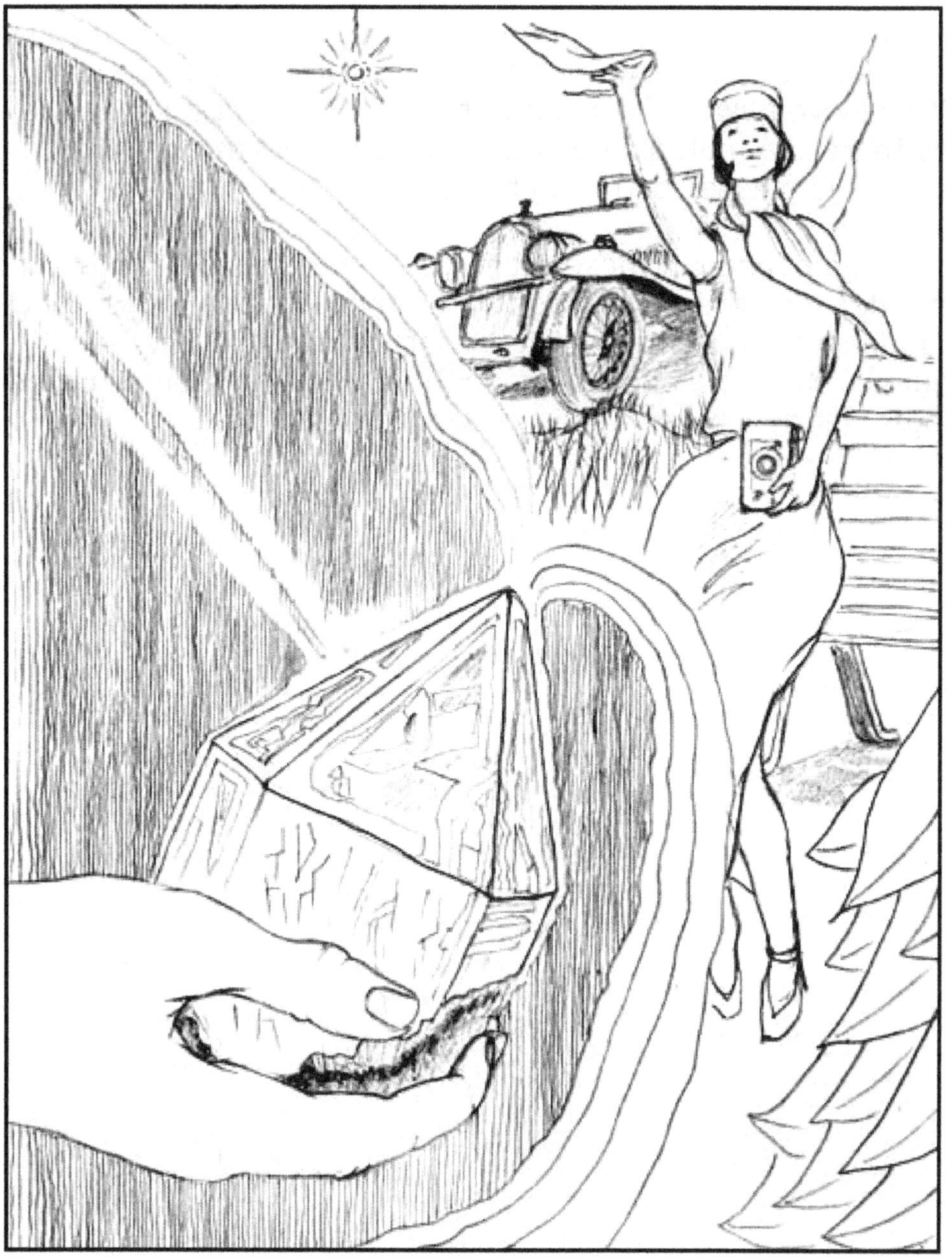

In a recent Elestial Crystal Gaze... I was invited by a charming lady to join the scene... but first she wanted to take my photo... so I posed, and enjoyed it... yes, I did... I get the feel of the time to be the 1920's... there is a very electric energy constantly in the air... and then she gently holds my arm and we stroll through the park... and I keep thinking about someone wanting a photo picture of me... are there psychic hooks from photos that others can pull at psychically?... that would explain a lot of sudden headaches...

I find out later that she's a non-lethal and non-hostile energy vampire... just a mild to strong flirtation that hooks you... and then you're feeding her that attention energy she wants/needs... you'll feel a little tired... but no harm will be done... it will even be done the favorite way you like it... if it doesn't hurt... well, not a lot anyway... as long as there is a mutual and equal exchange of astral energy that nourishes and pleases both... so be it...

Anything can happen in these realms... I have absolutely no outline... nor any idea how these drawings shall proceed... again this thing is just happening... and whatever it is that you really don't need to be happening... so, come and escape with us... meditate on or in the drawings... let go... flow with it ... just for the fun of it...

THIS LADY IS NOT THE MUSE... IT'S ANOTHER PERSON ALTOGETHER...

I have no idea where the Muse is... and this lady wants some attention and more than just taking my picture... she wants to pose for a portrait... and then she's inspired to take off all her clothes and to pose nude...'for the sake of art,' ...so, okay... I draw her naked...

NOW SHE POSES IN VARIOUS COSTUMES AND WIGS...

And then the Muse shows up... and lands her Lockheed P-38 Lightening that she's been flying around... they seem to know one another... and the Muse doesn't seemed too concerned about it... so, I just stay cool, sip my coffee, and keep on drawing...

SO, IT TURNS OUT THAT THEY ARE COUSINS...

Magdalene introduces the Lady as Maxine the Muse, her cousin who's specialty is erotic art inspirations. She senses my awkward feeling and assures me that being attracted to her is natural... she is after all an erotic art muse.

She further explains that while she and I have a spiritual/loving relationship with occasional sexual expressions... with Maxine it will probably be an erotic/loving relationship with a lot of sexual expressions... and not to worry about it because we're all connected and the love is unconditional... and I say, "well... okay..."

Then she explains that she has to go to St. Louis for a few days to a Muse Convention... and that she wants to try out her new airplane by flying it there. Then she's all excited and in a hurry and kisses us both and then gets into her Lockheed P-38 Lightening and flies off to St. Louis.

Maxine just smiles at me for a minute and then asks, "Did you want to draw me... some more?"

"Ah.... Yes... yes, I would...

She put on a 1950's pinup girl look... "The fifties were always my favorite years... everything was still naughty back then..."

"You Muse girls certainly keep your figures in good shape... yes... indeed..."

We're Goddesses... you silly..."

"Yes... I am the silly one...."

THE INFINITE POSSIBILITIES... OF THE MIND...

Maxine shows me some of the infinite possibilities... of the mind. She takes three different poses in different attire and at three different locations... all simultaneously! It's like watching three televisions... except that there are three sets of me watching the three TVs... and then our eyes meet and my mind starts doing multiplications of the infinite possibilities with such a lady... and it makes me dizzy... and that's probably why the drawing is a little funny...

FLOWING WITH IT... AND BEING IT...

It is an incredible place to reach in one's art... where the lines of reality blur... am I doing the drawing or the drawing doing me? ...Am I 'wishing' drawing her... or is she 'inspiring' drawing us.... or is it a mutual 'wish' happening for us both? ...I'm going to just give into this... and let this go where ever it's going to go... because it's feeling really nice...

GETTING MORE... AND TRYING TO GET IT ALL...

Artist pioneers like Michelangelo, Rembrandt, Lautrec, Picasso, and many others taught us how to abstract... to push, to stretch the usual boundaries of ordinary reality... and thus to create something that says even more from another reality...with lucid colors, dynamic movement, sounds, touch, smells, and tastes...

There is always more there... it's just a matter of tuning into it....

HOW TO MAKE A MUSE HAPPY...

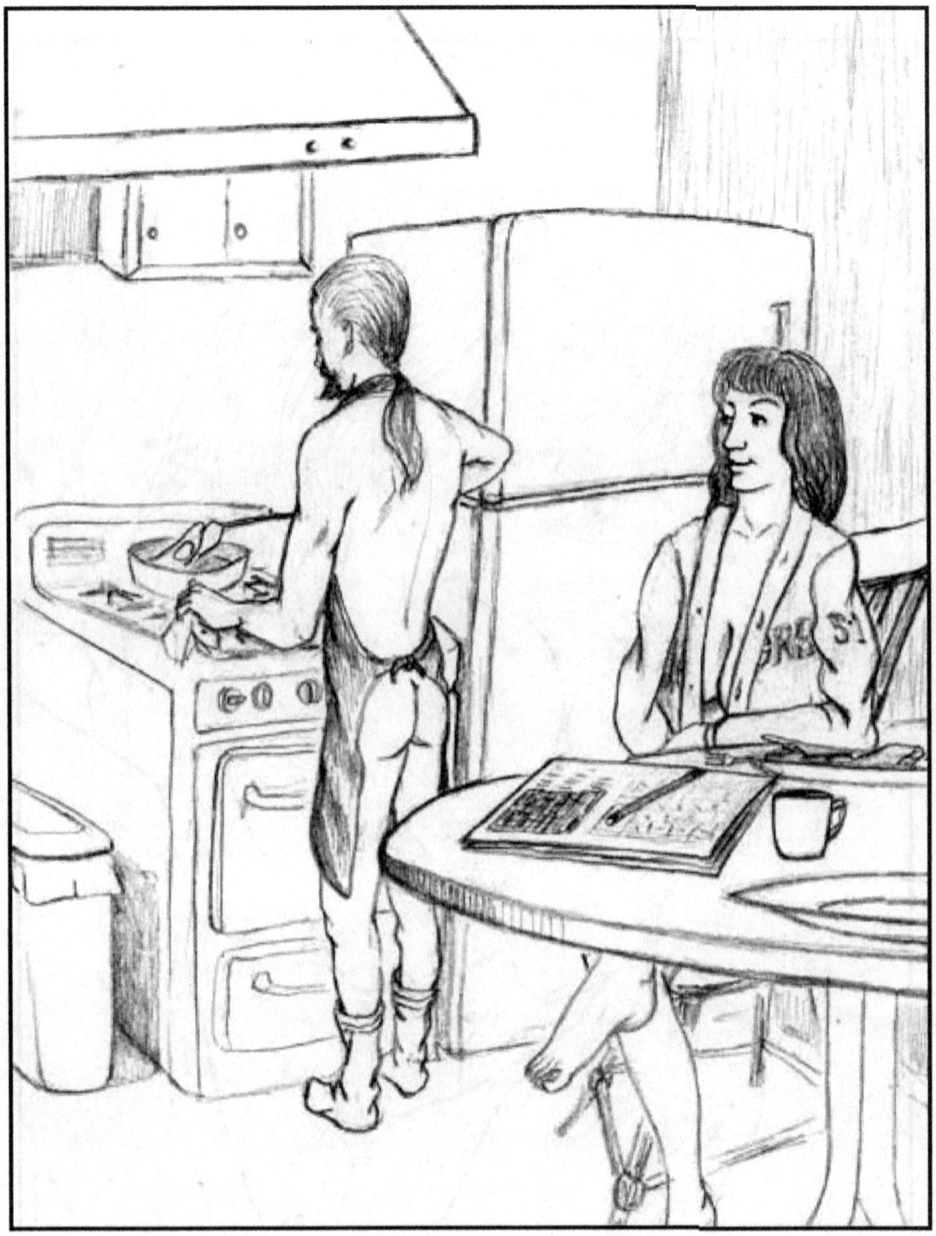

Have the morning newspaper folded and turned out to the crossword puzzle and the comics... lend her your baseball shirt for a robe... and then put on an apron and cook up some breakfast... eggs over easy, hash browns, sausage patties well done, buttered toast and strawberry preserves, and French roast coffee...

TIME TO GO OUT FOR AWHILE...

The Muses have other things to do... so, I'm on my own for now. I'm hungry, so I go down to a local diner and find all these happy young people there. People can be really nice when they're having a good time. We should all try and do that more often.

THE POSTURE OFTEN SPEAKS AS LOUD AS THE FACE...

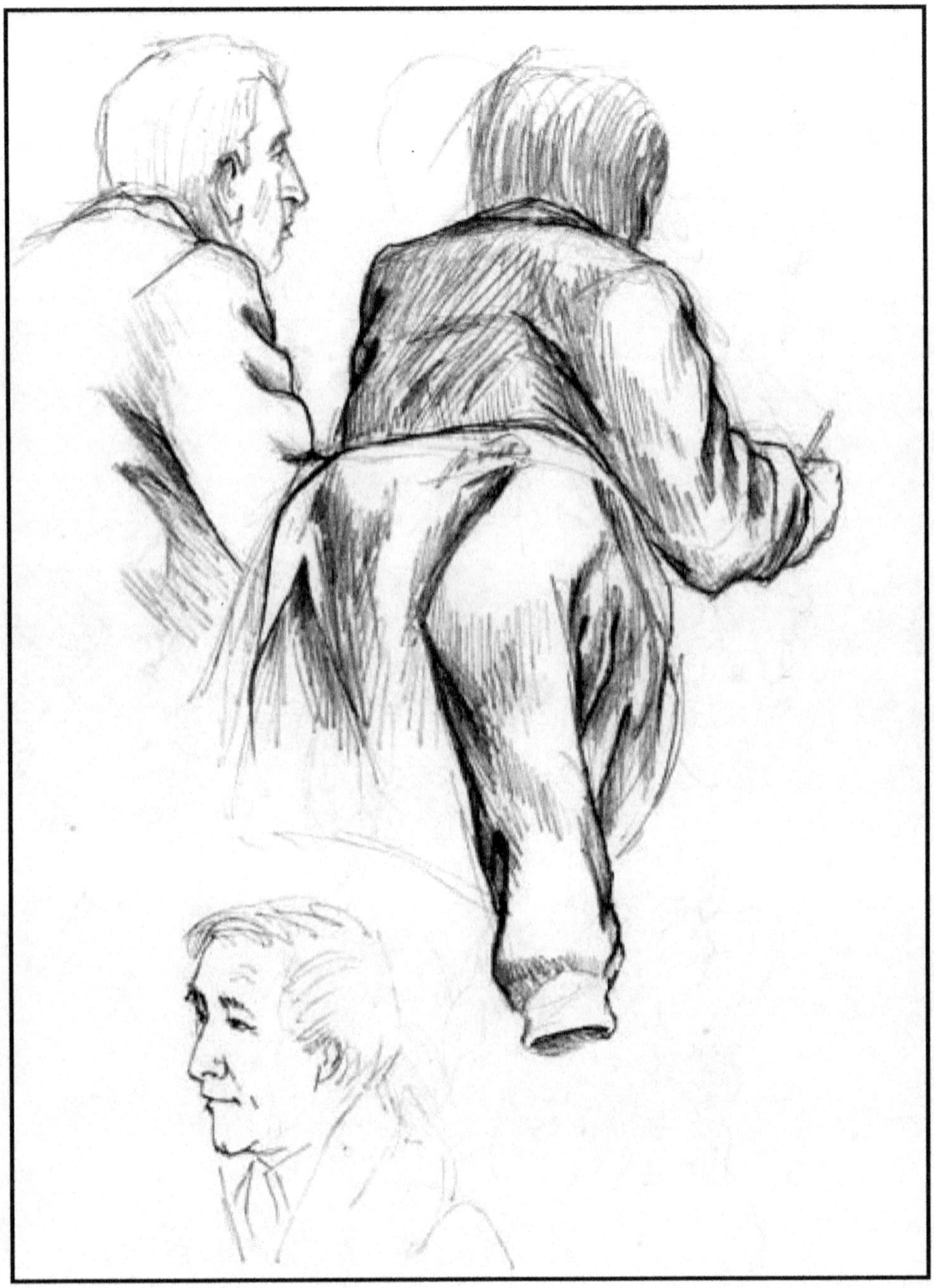

After the happy folks leave there's just these fellows left... who just look tired... run down... maybe bored... or depressed. The slouching, the tension in the shoulders, even the folds in the shirts and jackets, all have a downward depressed feeling. It's the same place, just thirty minutes later. What a difference a few happy people make.

DANCING PEOPLE ARE FUN TO DRAW...

Nightclubs and bars with dance floors are sometimes fun places to sketch. The main problem besides moving people is to find a spot with sufficient light to draw by. Gesture drawing is a style where one uses line to catch the movement or feel of a figure in motion without being overly concerned with accuracy of the drawing details. It's fun and good practice.

MEETINGS AND DRINKS AND CONVERSATION...

People meet in semi dark places, drink alcoholic beverages, and hopefully get relaxed enough to share some in depth honest communication,

"So... where are you from? ...originally?"

"Spokane..."

"Really! ...I have a cousin who lived there.."

A SHY AND QUICK MODEL...

While cleaning out some old files I found one of my early drawings from the 1960's. I can't remember my exact age. I think it was fourteen or fifteen. I was with my parents and we were driving around in the mountains and we stopped for a picnic lunch in the woods. Every few minutes this fellow would hop into view and then leave just as quickly. It was my first experience at sketching a moving model.

DRAWING ANOTHER ARTIST DRAWING PEOPLE...

It not a common occurrence outside of art school, but on occasion an artist will have the opportunity to sketch another artist sketching people. Makes one wonder about the parallel universe theories, fated encounters with others where there is mutual inspiration... or perhaps like energy attracting like energy... or just an odd coincidence.

Some different people

are in the coffee shop

this morning....

...and they all

want some caffeine...

...and some sugar...

and maybe just a smile

and a simple. 'hello,'

It's interesting to

find and draw

the very young...

...and the very

much older...

sitting in the same

environment... so

short... this adventure

of life.

A FELLOW WHO RADIATES CONFIDENCE...

I had an interesting conversation with this fellow. He is an independent electrical contractor. His entire business is in a truck van and he claims to always have more than enough work. He has an interesting philosophy of 'ONE' ...one business, one truck, one car, one house, one wife, and one child... and to take it all one day at a time.

A YOUNG WOMAN IN A VERY GOOD MOOD...

This young woman reminds me of the old rock and roll song CALIFORNIA GIRLS... the long wind blown hair, the shades, the confident 'fer sure,' smile and attitude.

No, I didn't get her phone number or a date... but she was a delightful 'model of the moment,' and she picked up this humble artist's check for a cheeseburger, fries, and coffee in exchange for a quick sketch.

A PRETTY YOUNG WOMAN... WITH A UNIQUE TAIL...

As we have seen, I get in these wandering moods for a few days until I find that one unique model... that just does it for me... I don't know how else to describe it. I reach a point where I've found whatever it was I went to find... and then it's time to go home and meditate and see what that brings on.

MY ELESTIAL CRYSTAL... A MEDITATION AND HEALING TOOL...

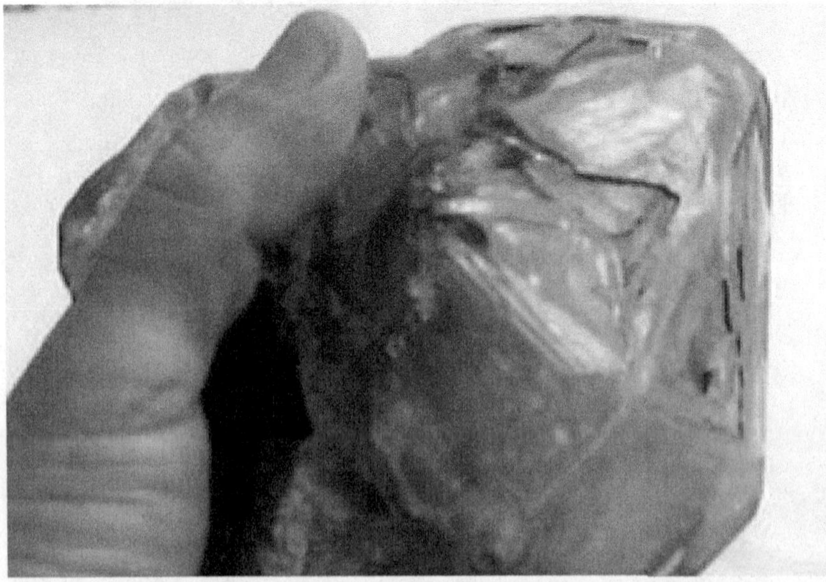

This is the Elestial Crystal that I described some pages back. To enter into a meditative or 'time travel,' state, I simply quiet my thoughts and gaze with a soft focus into one of the etched planes of the crystal's surface. The various points and planes present both still and moving pictures and in monochrome or color. The older scenes appear in sepia and/or black and white. The more recent scenes are in color.

Let's gaze into it... and see what happens...

THE GAZE GETS MORE PERSONAL...

This feels like a more in depth and personal vision... there are no structures or machines... just these few people... Am I watching this or am I participating? Nothing is very clear yet, just some vague images of figures are seen... we shall see what ideas develop from this

SOMETHING WANTS TO COME OUT... AND TO TELL HER STORY?

This face wants to come out... I think it's one of the many faces of Magdalene the Muse. What is she trying to tell/share with me? There are yet other figures inside the crystal... what are their roles in this vision quest? Scrying teaches one patience... you simply have to wait for the picture to form... there's no rushing it or, 'doing it.'

HONEST COMMUNICATION... IT IS POSSIBLE... DO YOU WANT IT?

We all complain about the lies of people and life. What if I could know your deepest thoughts and you could know mine? Would you want that? There a lot of people (especially the politicians and religious leaders of the world) who do not want that. Thus we are kept in the dark about many things.

FINDING EACH OTHER WITHIN EACH OTHER...

With guidance from the higher, and through unconditional love, and acceptance of each other, 'as is,' we can help each other find, experience, and own our inner nature which is usually the opposite or our physical gender. How do I see and experience myself through your eyes and body? ....and you, me?

OTHER PEOPLE'S ENERGY HAS AN EFFECT ON US...

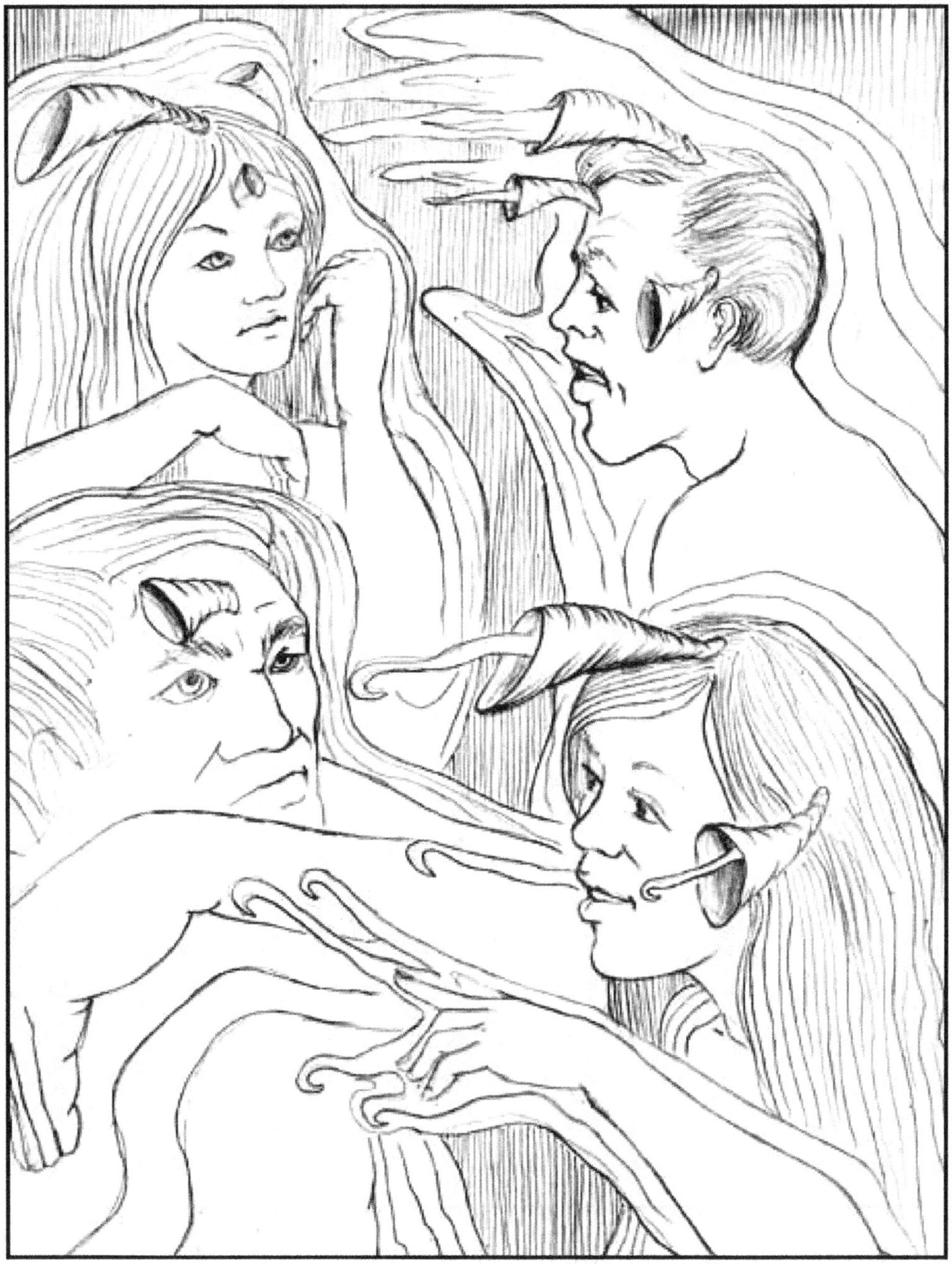

Sometimes we feel over whelmed by someone else's energy and we are suddenly just flowing along in their energy path with no control over our lives. Others seem to pull one into their lives and agendas and they keep you there with their various psychic hooks... and how often do we do the same to others?

FEELING DEPRESSED?...IT MAY BE SOMEONE ELSE'S NEGATIVITY...

Scientific research of telekinesis has proven that thought is an energy that can have an effect on physical matter. Your aura may be cluttered with other people's negativity. Angry thoughts of others can be like 'psychic darts,' which drains one's vitality. Forgiveness and making peace with others may actually be more practical common sense advice to redirect the other person's negativity to something else, other than a 'holy' or 'spiritual' act that makes one 'special.'

PSYCHIC SELF DEFENSE...

It is not difficult to defend oneself from negative psychic attack. One must be alert and aware of being under attack. Any sudden mood swing, pain, discomfort, anxiety... with no apparent cause in your environment can be an alert signal that one is under the influence of another's negativity coming toward you.

Step back from yourself, and try to listen to your rambling thoughts. You hear them in your own voice and they are fearful, angry, even violent... but are they your thoughts? Yes, you listen and you hear them... but, the thoughts are in your own voice! This is where we are often fooled. We assume that if it's our voice it must be our thought. We are 'creatures of habit' and the majority of the time we go about hearing our own voice when thinking.

To better see what I mean try this experiment... mentally hear with the voice of one of your favorite film stars or another person's voice that you know well...

I found that all of a sudden I'm hearing Humphrey Bogart whining and complaining, "you're a lousy operator!" He's complaining about my job performance... Then I see it. I am insecure about my job performance... I am assuming my voice to be his thought! It's not my thought! It's not Bogie's thought! It's Jack's thought... and he says that about all of the operators! He's a jerk and the boss knows it! ...now I'm feeling better...

However, you get there... you suddenly realize someone's negativity is draining you. It is a simple matter of grounding oneself. I visualize roots going down from my feet deep into the ground. Then draw bright light down through the crown chakra from your higher self... some say guardian angels... names don't matter... just know that you have a higher force that you may call on at any time and that it is as strong as anyone else's. As you breathe in see this light filling up your aura and as you breathe out, any negative deposits are being drained through the roots and recycled through mother earth

Using symbols that have meaning for you, such as crossing oneself, or hand parries are effective defense. Another powerful and simple defense is to turn and face the thought and firmly say mentally or out loud if you're alone, "I deny you!"

If you're interested in psychic phenomenon most any new age bookstore will a half a dozen or so books on the subject of psychic attack and self defense methods.

LET'S TAKE AN ESPRESSO BREAK FROM ALL THIS HEAVY STUFF...

I found these old drawings that I did in Europe from early 1970's. Here I have used felt tip pen and then I applied a wash shadow from a #00 sable brush. dipped in a cup of espresso. It was an interesting effect, and an attention getting trick to attract viewer/customers to my café table studio of the evening... Those were fun times.

ESPRESSO DRAWING...

Another crowd gathering trick as a public sketch artist was to put the pen away and then to dip the brush into the thick dregs of the espresso and then to draw with just the brush and espresso. This drawing is now 36 years old!... that was some strong espresso back then...

AN OCCASIONAL FIGURE MODEL IS ALWAYS A DELIGHT...

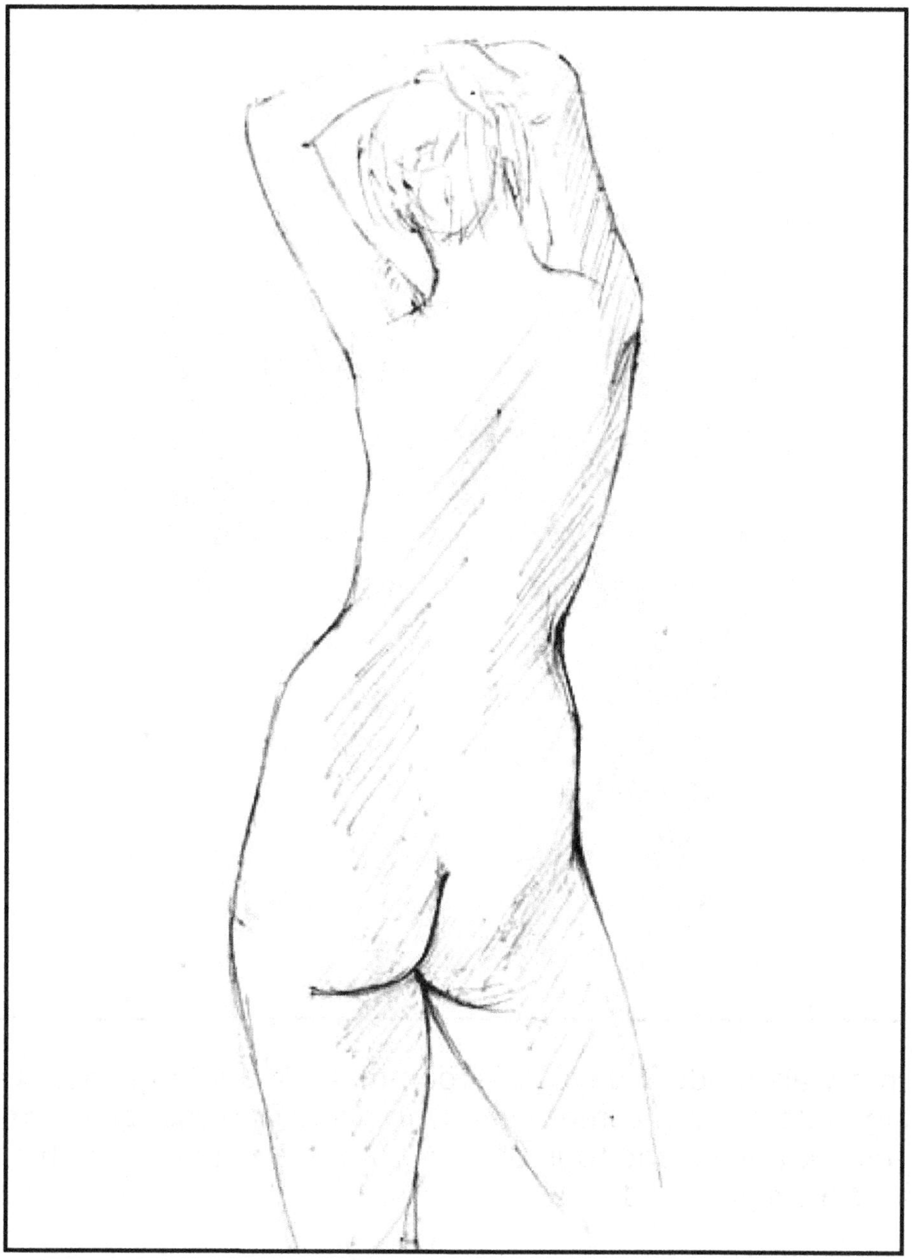

Once in a while you get lucky and some lovely lady is inspired to take off her clothes and to model nude, 'for the sake of art.' ...It's not so bad... you learn to flow with it... it's all good public relations... and good advertising...and good exposure, etc., etc.

YEA, VERILY...MY CUP RUNNETH ORE...

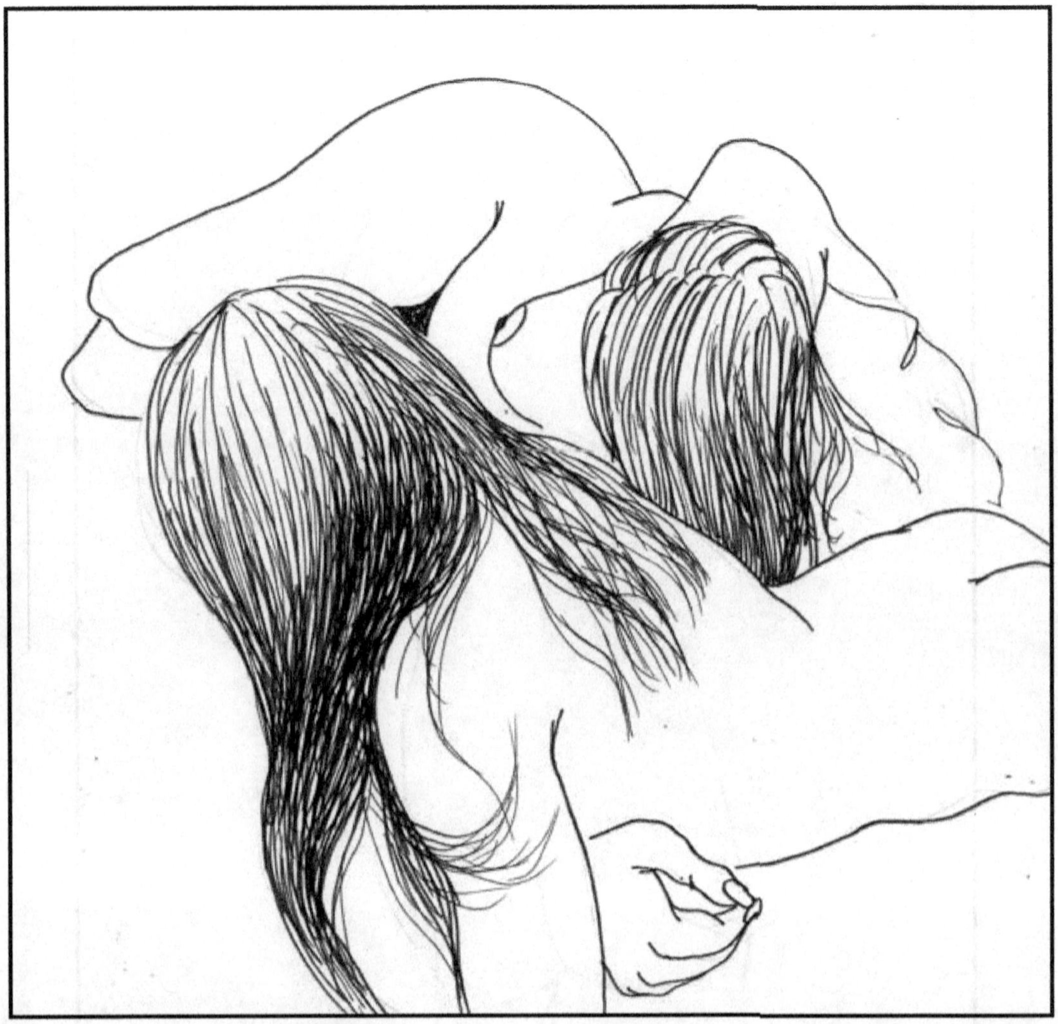

Once, in my art student days, the roommate of a young coed who was modeling nude for me, came home from work and thought it would be fun to join in, and so she took off her clothes and did... and this is one of those drawings from 1974.

I kept my cool and continued to draw while inwardly I am rejoicing, 'Yes! There is a God! ...Halleluiah!'

...the good life, a large pepperoni and mushroom pizza, a bottle of wine, a little herb... and two nude models... now ain't life grand!

WHEN YOU WANT A BREAK FROM PEOPLE... GO TO THE ZOO...

For a while in the spring of 1972 drawings of animals were selling well at the park where some of us artists sold our work. So, you have to spend a day at the Frankfurt A.M., West Germany Zoo drawing up some inventory. Most of them sold very quickly. I only have six of those drawings from that day that have survived over the years.

The bears were always popular and sold well.

A LAZY AFTERNOON WITH THE LIONS...

The Lions always sold well... and they were easy to draw... because they slept most of the time...

THERE IS NO PROBLEM FINDING INTERESTING SUBJECTS...

In a good zoo you will find fascinating models around every corner....
and they will remind you of people you know!

A VERY POWERFUL FELLOW YOU DON'T WANT TO MESS WITH...

In European zoos the visitor can stand much closer to the cages, in this drawing within three feet or so, than one can in most American zoos. The European attitude being more, 'if you're dumb enough to stick you hand in there you deserve to get it torn off..' He seemed to be in a mellow mood and didn't mind posing... but.. that close I could feel from his mere presence or aura... his incredible strength! Imagine meeting this fellow in the wild on his turf... and he can out run you, catch you, and tear your head off.

A CHEERFUL AND UPBEAT FELLOW...

I caught these two in the same view because their habitats were next to one another. As the elephant trumpeted and pranced about he seemed to be saying, "Hello there, art fellow... toss us some peanuts?... don't mind Ralph Rhino there... he's just in a mood... shall I pose straight on... or perhaps a profile? I'm easy..."

THE JAQUZZI IS GETTING A LITTLE CROWDED...

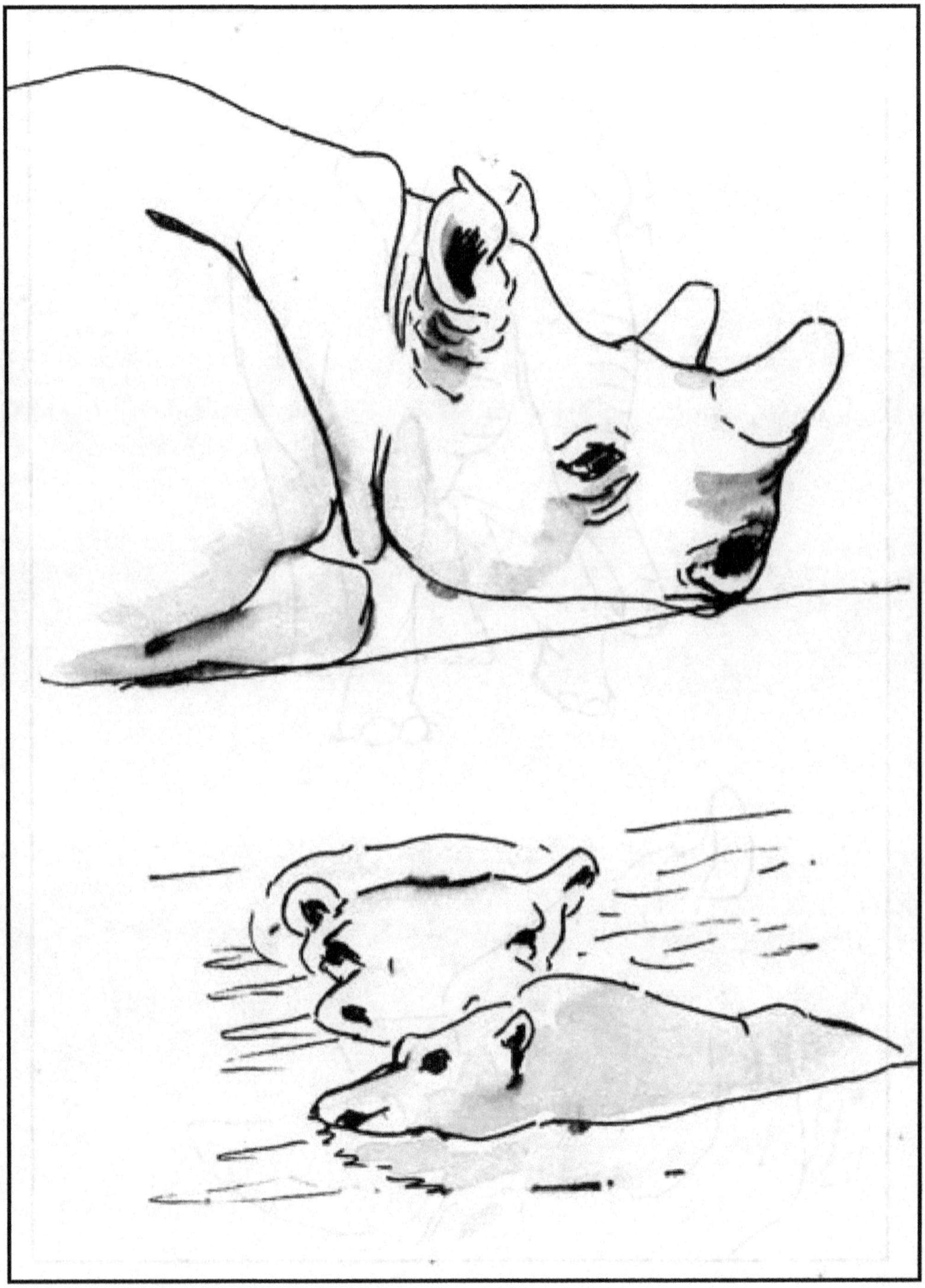

What does one say to a couple of Hippopotamuses who are taking up all the room... "Do you mind moving over just a bit... thank you..."

THE NUDE POET READS TO ME...

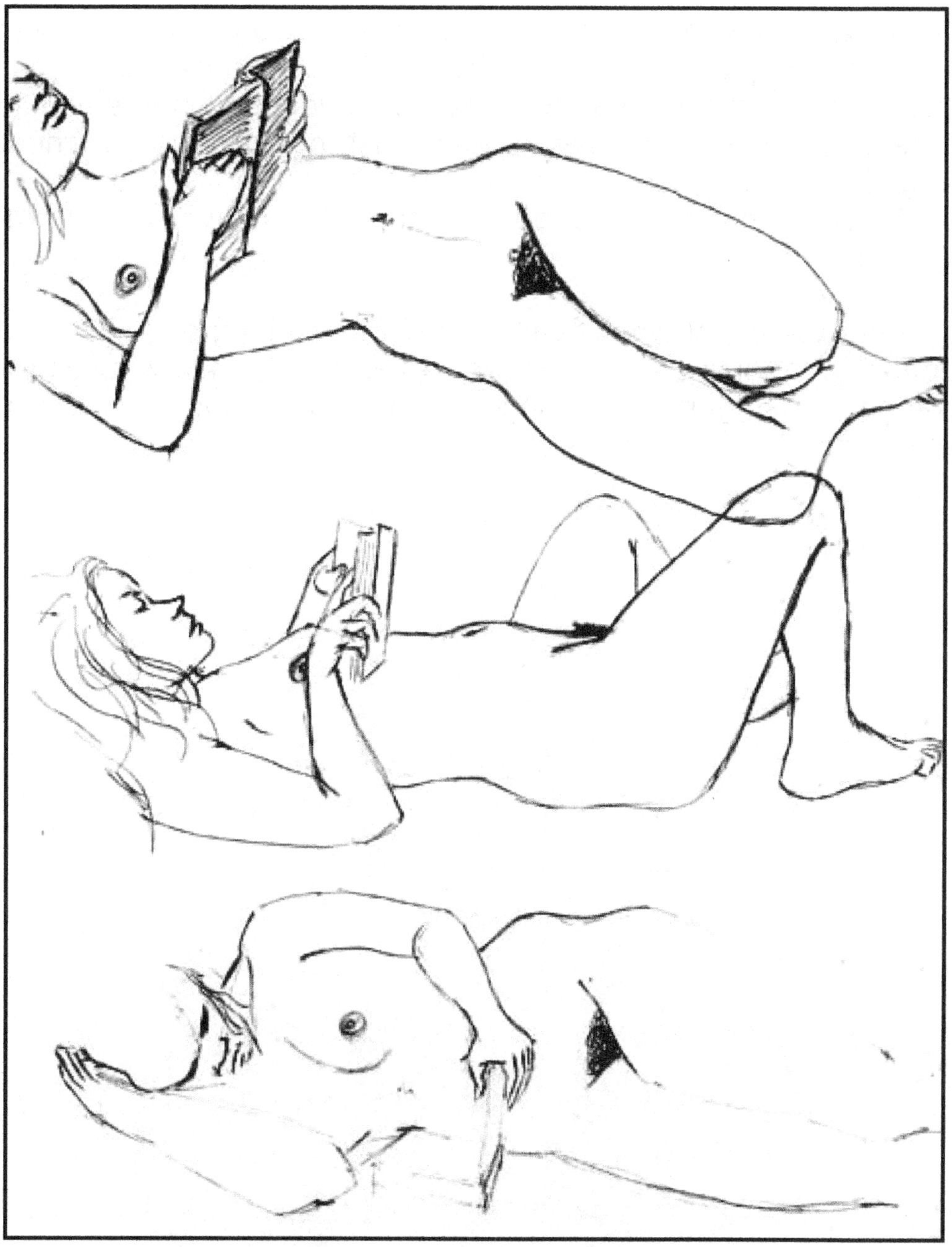

Why did I draw three views of her on the same page? I just got caught up in the poems she was reading to me and I forgot to turn the page. Artists, writers, musicians, and many creative people in general are just quirky that way.

When studying art history during my college years I always sought out pictures of the artist's sketch books and portfolios. When you look at a painting or a statue you are seeing the finished work as delivered to the patron. In that work you are only seeing one part of the artist.

In the sketches leading up to the finished work you can see how the artist thinks and plans the work... the rough quick lines, the notes, the re-draws, the composition angles... some smudges, coffee stains (or wine, tea, just whatever beverage the artist indulges in) ...all there... and unpolished... and these 'think pages,' can often tell you more about the artist than the finished work that they deliver to a patron to pay the rent.

Here is an example of what I call an artist's 'thinking page,' from one of Leonardo De Vinci's sketch books. As an artist, I know exactly what he's doing. He's figuring out the position of the hands that he wants to paint.

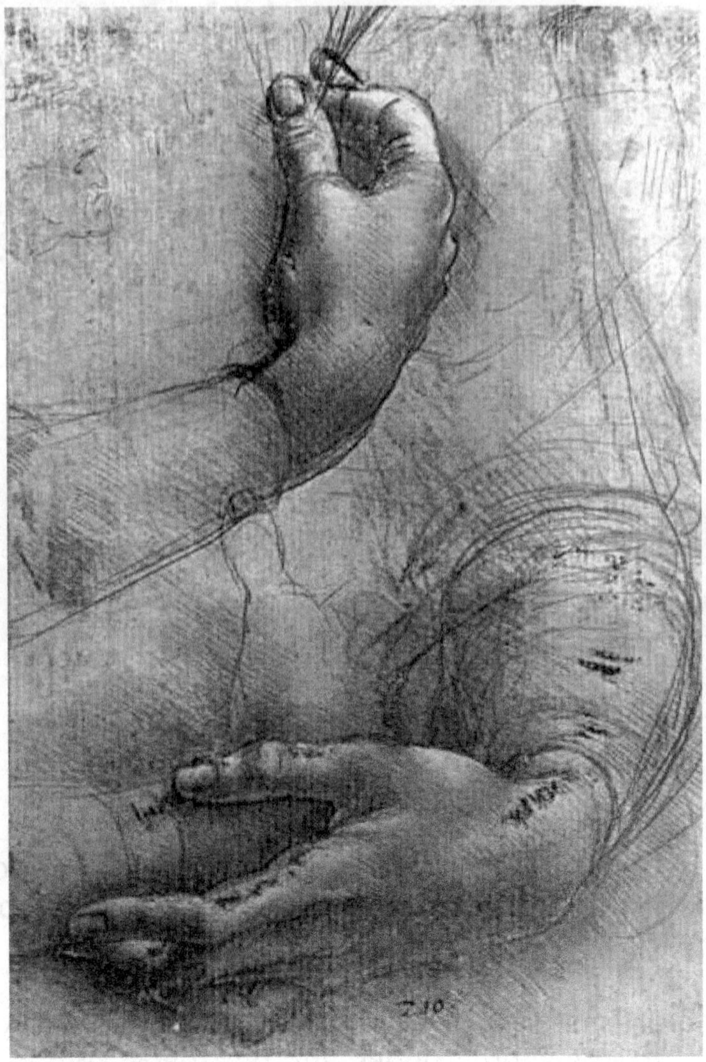

From Leonardo De Vinci – study of hands

Look closely at the details. One can see the left hand is holding a lightly sketched in right hand. I can almost hear his thoughts, '..no... that's boring... maybe, if I have the right hand reach up... yes, and fidget with a necklace or broach, button, or something... yes, that's more natural...' ...and then he draws the right hand in detail, not bothering with erasing or rubbing off the previous hand that he had started. You can see 'scratch lines' at the upper right side where he sharpened his pencil and was testing the line. There appear to be a few drops or liquid stains here and there from whatever he was drinking at the moment, and smudges of dirt from being stacked on the drafting table or tossed into a storage portfolio.

The irony... Leonardo never meant for anyone to see this... it's just a rough studio sketch he did while working on a painting, and today it hangs in a museum, framed, insured, guarded, and is worth hundreds of thousands of dollars... maybe even millions.

ME AND LEONARDO DE VINCI... SAME PROCESS...

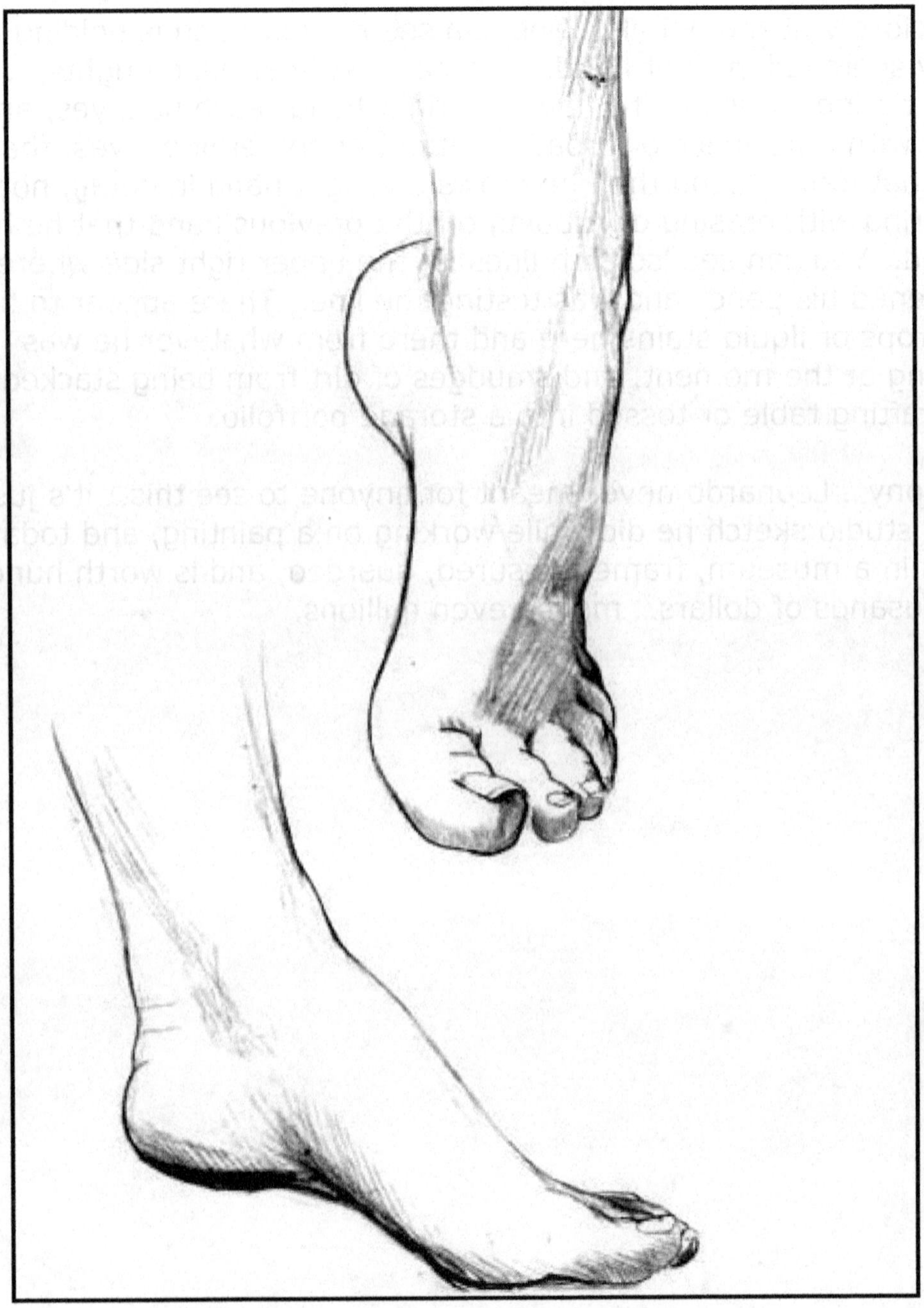

Two different artists... different eras... same problems. When you're having trouble with a particular part of the human anatomy you go do some detailed close up drawings of it to figure it out. This is a studio work sketch from years ago. It was not intended to be a finished work... but when other viewers say otherwise, you frame it and offer it for sale or publish it. The difference between me and Leonardo is he didn't have a scanner and a Photoshop computer program to clean up the smudges and coffee stains.

A BEAUTIFUL MODEL WHO WILL POSE FOR CHICKEN FEED...

I spent the afternoon with my daughter at the Los Angeles Arboretum in Arcadia, California. At the patio coffee shop there the Peacocks are as common as Sparrows and Pigeons. They're so accustomed to people that some of them will eat from your hand. It cost me most of my large oatmeal cookie... but I managed to get a nice pose from this handsome young fellow.

LATER WE STOP AT A DINER... AND I CATCH SOME PEOPLE...

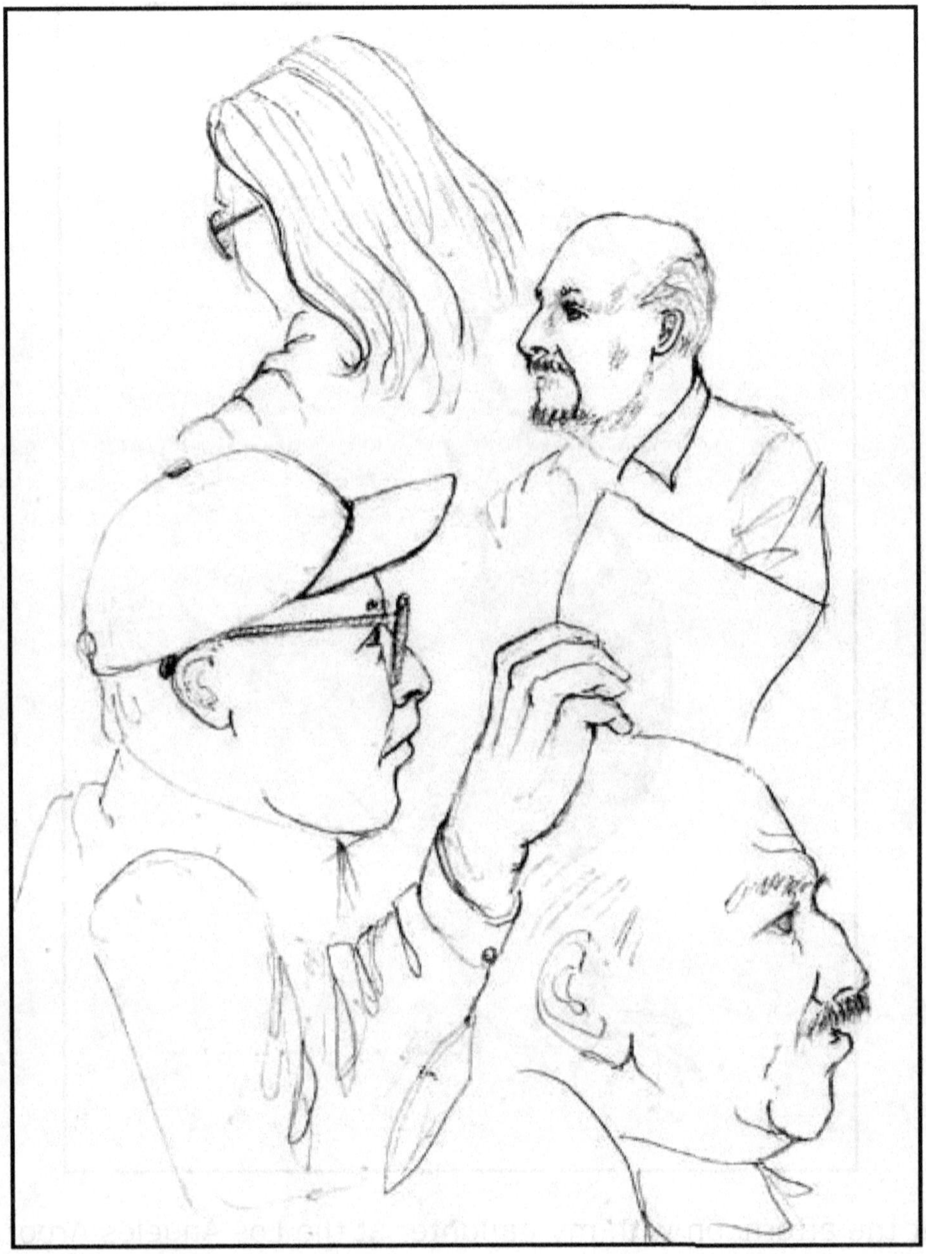

Each person in their own reality of feeling, thought, and being... yet somehow connected and all the same. The constant flipping back and forth from moments of consciousness and awareness of oneself in the midst of it all... versus long moments, even months and years sometimes, of walking sleep and just being part of the crowd.

WE'RE ALL MORE CONNECTED THAN WE CARE TO ADMIT...

Most of us have had more than one psychic experience where you just knew something about some one... or some event... If we would make more efforts to develop those finer senses... lies would no longer be possible... and perhaps true world peace could be achieved.

THERE ARE MANY DOORS IN THE MANSION OF THE MIND...

Some people are clairvoyant and see pictures. Some hear voices and are clairaudient, some just 'know,' through clairsentience... and some through emotions and empathy can feel others and their surrounding environment. We have many psychic centers and possibilities if we have an open mind and are fearless enough to explore our minds.

COMMUNICATING FROM A HIGHER PLACE... WORKS BETTER...

If the lower chakras are trying to speak for the heart and those messages are then sent on to the logical thinking... we have the usual relationship quagmire. If we start with listening to the higher center in us... literally 18 to 24 inches above the head, and some say residence of the guardian angels... and then let that influence work down through us and fill the heart chakra... often, if we are quiet... we will suddenly just 'know' if the relationship is 'right' for us or not.

THERE IS A PICTURE EVERYWHERE...

I found another drawing from my art school days. I was waiting for a girlfriend to get ready to go out... and so, I sat there... and so, I may as well draw her cozy single apartment while I wait. Some times it comes out the best, and you have the most fun... with the ones like this one... when you're just goofing around.

SPENDING TIME AGAIN ON THAT STRANGE STREET...

There is a six to eight block area of South Pasadena where either the streets are haunted, or there is a time warp back to the 1940's, or there is something about the neighborhood that triggers these images from my subconscious. For a few seconds I see these jumbled scenes... but not every time. However, it has been often enough so that I go back with my sketch book and wait for it to happen again.

THERE IS ALWAYS MORE TO BE SEEN...

I will admit that this was drawn after the fact from memory. This past August a young woman in her twenties was enjoying the apartment building pool. I was sitting on the other side of the pool sketching some plants. She was walking in the shadows at the side of the building. As I glanced up my eyes made a change of focus and for a few seconds I observed a bluish white aura that followed her movement. Various shapes swirled around her inside this space that surrounded her. From my research of this phenomenon, I knew I was seeing her aura and some of her thought forms. Then it all vanished as quickly as it had appeared. That's the tricky part... staying focused.

DID YOU EVER HAVE REPTITIOUS THOUGHTS?

On another occasion at the counter of a dimly lit (from a burned out light bulb overhead) diner an aura appeared around this fellow and repetitious shapes of thought forms came forth and floated about as if caught in a gentle swirling wind. I didn't know what his thoughts were ... but he definitely had something troublesome on or in his mind.

A QUIET MOMENT IN THE MORNING AND A CUP OF JAVA...

Millions of us begin our Monday morning at a counter or a side booth somewhere in some donut and coffee shop... sipping at a styrofoam cup of hot coffee, clearing out the cobwebs, waking up, and getting ready to meet whatever the day may bring. Do you know this fellow... is it you?

A CHANGE IN WEATHER BRINGS OUT THE FUNNY HATS AND CAPS...

In October the air is cold and crisp in the mornings and late evenings and you begin to see people changing to their heavier and warmer wardrobe... and putting on their funny hats.

AND AFTER THE DAY OF WORK IS DONE... RELAX AND HAVE A DRINK.

I found some old bar drawings from the late 1980's. About the only change I see in people are the usual hair changes... shorter or longer... and of course the cost of living and the price of drinks... continues to go ever upward.

AH, YES... THERE SHE IS... THE PRETTY ONE...

As is my habit... I wander around for a couple of days sketching here and there until I catch that one pretty profile that just does it... for me ...and then I go home.

TIME TO PUBLISH PORTFOLIO II... AND THEN TAKE A BREAK...

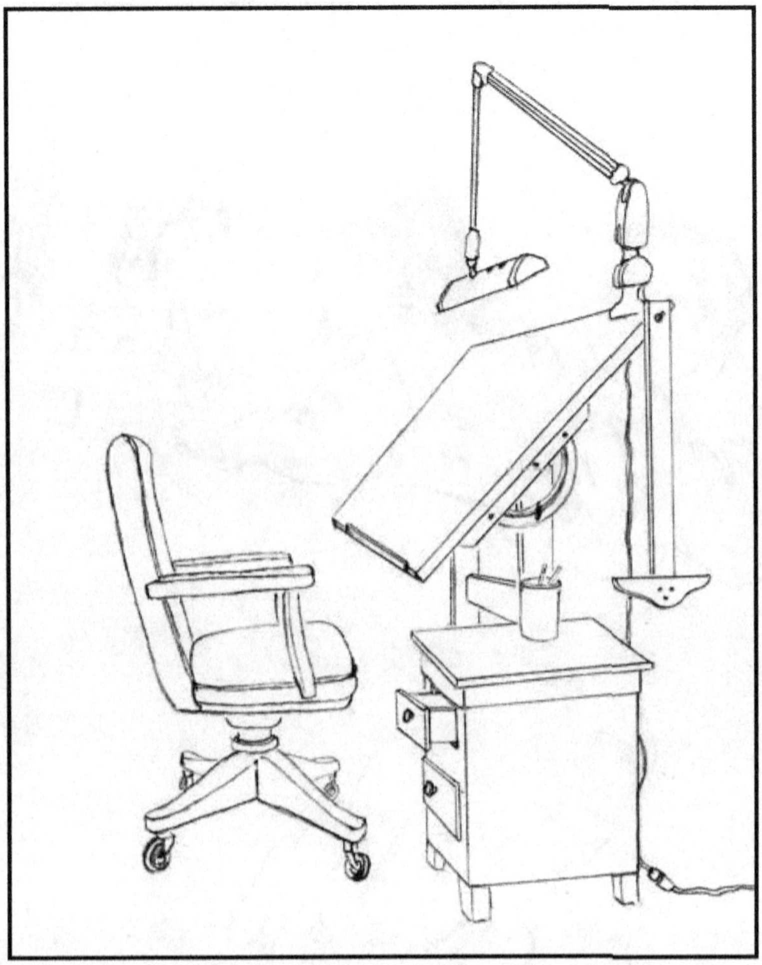

As I look back over the daily entries of the past few months, I surprise even myself at the various things we've explored. From our ordinary daily reality... the coffee shops, diners, bars, zoo, parks... on through inner doors in the mansion of our minds, and with our awareness we've crossed morph bridges to other dimensions and parallel realities. We've explored scrying (meditative gazing) as a method of mental and astral travel. Again I have used drawing as therapy, this time to cope with and accept the passing of my mother this past June. As an artist, I am simply a conduit that this marvelous energy flows through ...just a lucky guy who gets to hold on to the pencil and go along for the ride.

The Muse Magdalene is back... and she's talking about more doors, stairs, and bridges... Portfolio III should be interesting and we hope that you will join us for more inner and cosmic explorations.

Made in the USA
Monee, IL
14 September 2026

63198308R00083